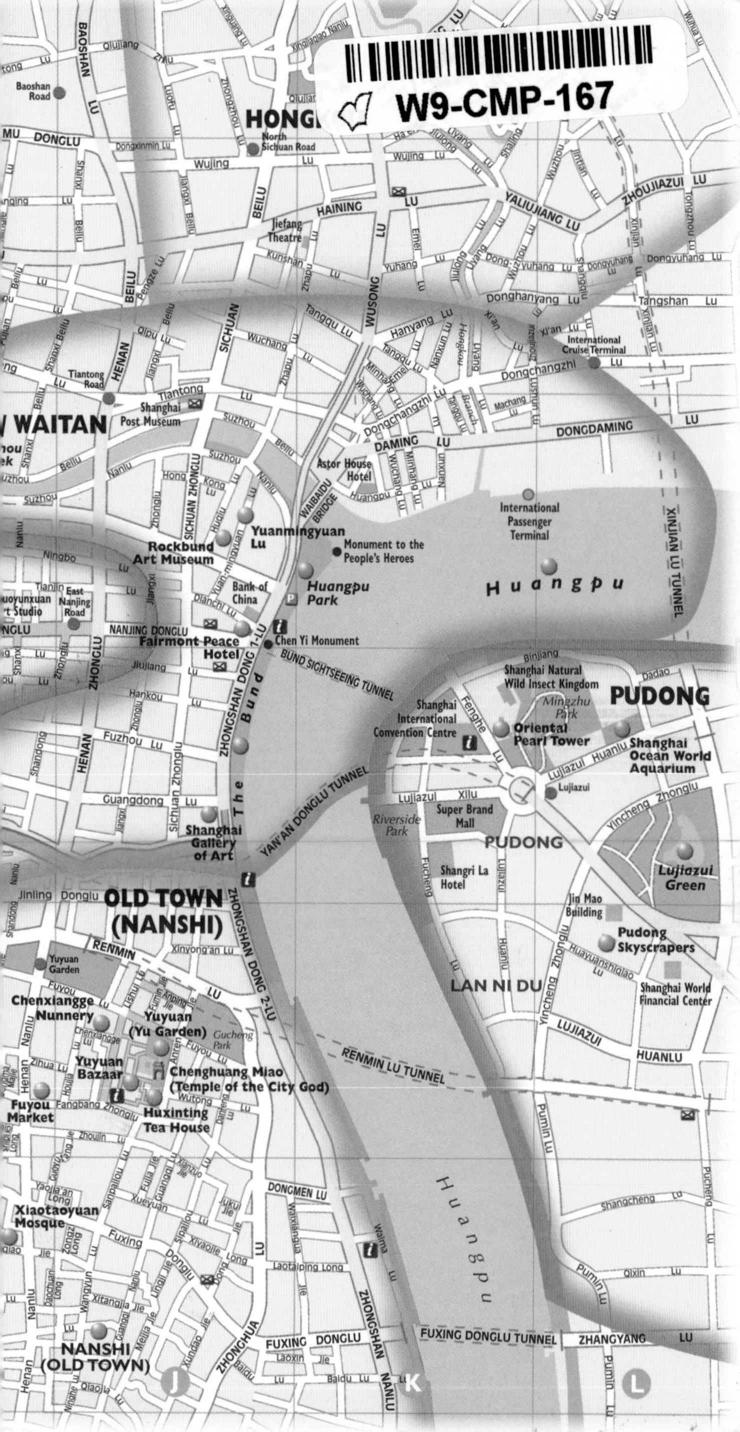
HONGKOU
North Sichuan Road
Baoshan Road
Jiefang Theatre
WAITAN
Tiantong Road
Shanghai Post Museum
Astor House Hotel
WAIBAIDU BRIDGE
Yuanmingyuan Lu
Rockbund Art Museum
Monument to the People's Heroes
Huangpu Park
Bank of China
East Nanjing Road
NANJING DONGLU
Fairmont Peace Hotel
Chen Yi Monument
BUND SIGHTSEEING TUNNEL
The Bund
ZHONGSHAN DONG 1-LU
International Passenger Terminal
International Cruise Terminal
Huangpu
DONGDAMING LU
XINJIAN LU TUNNEL
Shanghai Natural Wild Insect Kingdom
Mingzhu Park
PUDONG
Shanghai International Convention Centre
Oriental Pearl Tower
Shanghai Ocean World Aquarium
Lujiazui
Super Brand Mall
Riverside Park
Shangri La Hotel
Lujiazui Green
Jin Mao Building
Pudong Skyscrapers
Shanghai World Financial Center
LAN NI DU
YAN'AN DONGLU TUNNEL
Shanghai Gallery of Art
OLD TOWN (NANSHI)
ZHONGSHAN DONG 2-LU
Yuyuan Garden
Chenxiangge Nunnery
Yuyuan (Yu Garden)
Gucheng Park
Yuyuan Bazaar
Chenghuang Miao (Temple of the City God)
Huxinting Tea House
Fuyou Market
RENMIN LU TUNNEL
DONGMEN LU
Xiaotaoyuan Mosque
Huangpu
NANSHI (OLD TOWN)
FUXING DONGLU
FUXING DONGLU TUNNEL
ZHANGYANG LU
J
K
L

Fodor's

25 Best

SHANGHAI

How to Use This Book

KEY TO SYMBOLS

- Map reference to the accompanying fold-out map
- Address
- Telephone number
- Opening/closing times
- Restaurant or café
- Nearest rail station
- Nearest subway (Metro) station
- Nearest bus route
- Nearest riverboat or ferry stop
- Facilities for visitors with disabilities
- Other practical information
- Further information
- Tourist information
- Admission charges:
  Expensive (more than 50RMB)
  Moderate (20–50RMB)
  Inexpensive (20RMB or less)

This guide is divided into four sections

- Essential Shanghai: An introduction to the city and tips on making the most of your stay.
- Shanghai by Area: We've broken the city into seven areas, and recommended the best sights, shops, entertainment venues, nightlife and restaurants in each one. Suggested walks help you to explore on foot. Farther Afield takes you beyond the center.
- Where to Stay: The best hotels, whether you're looking for luxury, budget or something in between.
- Need to Know: The information you need to make your trip run smoothly, including getting about by public transportation, weather tips, emergency phone numbers and useful websites.

Navigation In the Shanghai by Area chapter, we've given each area its own color, which is also used on the locator maps throughout the book and the map on the inside front cover.

Maps The fold-out map with this book is a comprehensive street plan of Shanghai. The grid on this fold-out map is the same as the grid on the locator maps within the book. We've given grid references within the book for each sight and listing.

Contents

Introducing Shanghai

One of the world's great cities, Shanghai is China's dynamic window on the future. A dazzling hybrid of old and new, East and West, communist and capitalist, Shanghai is in a constant state of reinvention. Prepare to be wowed.

The Shanghainese themselves would likely tell you that Shanghai is the fastest-changing city in the world—and that's before the city has properly hit its stride.

The blend of urban enormity, a vast and dense population, a swirl of fuming traffic, as well as a here-today, gone-tom-orrow mentality, can make Shanghai a tricky city to get a handle on. The city's commitment to its past (the Bund, the French Concession) and its future (Pudong) creates a sensation of time moving in two directions, while a frenetically busy population of white-collar workers and the industrious middle classes generates a blur of activity that seldom slows. Shanghai is rarely, if ever, unexciting.

But if you slow the pace yourself to wander through the leafy lanes of the French Concession or track down the city's art deco heritage, you can put the brakes on this fast-moving metropolis and sample its more sedate side. And when you are ready for a further lift, you can speed to one of the highest observation towers in the world for extraordinary views over this breathtaking city. If the view across China's city-of-the-future really captures your imagination, some stratospheric hotels offer round-the-clock panoramas as standard.

Shanghai has some of China's top sights, from the Shanghai Museum to the Bund and the skyscrapers of Pudong. And in its quest to blow the socks off other cities in China, food, drink and entertainment have also received due attention. Shanghai's bars, restaurants and nightclubs are among the most inventive, and most copied, in the land.

FACTS AND FIGURES

- The resident population of Shanghai is estimated to exceed 24 million.
- In 2017, Shanghai's GDP grew to US$469 billion, expanding at a rate of almost 7%.
- There are more than 50,000 taxis in the city.
- An estimated 174,000 expats live in Shanghai.

HIGH SOCIETY

Until 1983, the Park Hotel on Nanjing Lu was the tallest building in Shanghai and, until 1963, was the tallest building in the land. That seems hard to believe now, when the Park Hotel is dwarfed by skyscrapers. Across the Huangpu River, in Pudong, are some of the tallest structures on the planet, including the Shanghai Tower, the world's second-tallest building.

ART DECO

Shanghai is a treasure trove of art deco architecture, particularly around Nanjing Lu and in Luwan and Xuhui. Surviving the turmoil of the 20th century, these hotels, apartments, banks and theaters are a riveting roll call of 1920s and 1930s machine age. Classic examples are the Fairmont Peace Hotel, the Cathay Theatre and 1933, a deco slaughterhouse in Hongkou.

RIDING HIGH

Maglev (Magnetic Levitation) trains run between Pudong International Airport and Longyang Road Metro station. At a top speed of 267mph (430kph), the trains complete the 19-mile (30.5km) journey in under 8 minutes. Plans for a 109-mile (175km) Shanghai–Hangzhou Maglev line were reportedly shelved after a high-speed rail link opened in 2010.

A Short Stay in Shanghai

DAY 1

Morning Start with arguably the city's best breakfast in the **Grand Brasserie** at the luxurious Waldorf Astoria (▷ 66) in the heart of colonial Shanghai, then walk along **the Bund** (▷ 58–59) and the waterfront, looking over to Pudong.

Mid-morning Head for **Yuyuan** (Yu Garden; ▷ 74) in the Old Town, then relax over a pot of Chinese tea in the Huxinting Tea House (▷ 70–71, 79) or the Old Shanghai Tea House (▷ 79).

Lunch Aim for the **Nan Xiang** (▷ 79) for servings of Chinese *xiaolongbao* (dumplings; ▷ 66), but you may have to wait in line. Or sample one of the Chinese snacks at the plentiful stalls in the **Yuyuan Bazaar** (▷ 76).

Afternoon Wander the narrow streets of the **Old Town** (▷ 72–73), with their popular dumpling restaurants and antiques and jewelry shops.

Mid-afternoon Stroll through **People's Square** (▷ 40–41) and the neighboring **People's Park** (▷ 38–39). Take in the outstanding bronzes, porcelain and paintings in the **Shanghai Museum** (▷ 42–43).

Dinner Have a table reserved on the terrace of **M on the Bund** (▷ 66) for dramatic Pudong nighttime views. Afterward, walk off your meal along the Bund promenade, gazing over to the neonscape across the water and finding the best angle on Shanghai's ultimate photo op.

Evening Catch an acrobatics performance at the **Shanghai Centre Theatre** (▷ 50), or a live-music show, followed by drinks in a French Concession bar (▷ 24–25).

DAY 2

Morning Have breakfast at the Austrian-themed **Baker & Spice** (▷ 32), before visiting **Tianzifang** (▷ 28) to explore its small shops and appealing shikumen architecture. Begin to explore the French Concession's intriguing historical buildings, such as the **Moller Villa**, **St. Nicholas Church** and the **Shanghai Arts & Crafts Museum** (▷ 30).

Mid-morning Stay in the stylish **French Concession** (▷ 24–25) to browse its chic boutiques and snappy shops, before taking the Metro to Lujiazui to climb to the observation decks of the **Jin Mao Tower** (▷ 94), the **Shanghai World Financial Center** (▷ 94) or the **Shanghai Tower** (▷ 94) for memorable city views.

Lunch Enjoy a memorable meal at **Jade on 36** (▷ 96), in Tower Two of the Pudong Shangri-La, or choose from the three kitchens of **On 56** (▷ 96) in the good-looking Jin Mao Tower.

Afternoon Go for a cruise on the **Huangpu River** (▷ 60–61), passing through the port area as far as the confluence with the Yangtze River.

Dinner Head to **Xintiandi** (▷ 44) to explore the distinctive sights and peruse the shops before dining at **T8** (▷ 52), but make sure you reserve a table as its high-class reputation makes it a popular choice. After your meal, have a drink in a Xintiandi bar or stroll through the surrounding streets to soak up the atmosphere.

Evening Take the Metro to **People's Square** (▷ 40–41) for a drink in **Barbarossa** (▷ 50) and enjoy some staggering nighttime views of the surrounding skyscrapers and walk along the bustling, neon length of Nanjing Road.

Top 25

TOP 25

Around Suzhou Creek ⊳ **56–57** Former consulates and grand old Shanghai mansions.

The Bund ⊳ **58–59** Shanghai's splendid embankment is lined with renovated 1920s buildings.

Duolun Lu Cultural Street ⊳ **84–85** A historic street, lined with shops and old houses.

Yuyuan ⊳ **74** The finest classical garden in Shanghai and the city's most popular tourist sight.

Xujiahui Cathedral ⊳ **29** Catholic cathedral easily recognizable by its twin spires and redbrick facade.

Xintiandi ⊳ **44** A glamorous collection of shops, entertainment venues and restaurants in restored and rebuilt traditional shikumen houses.

Urban Planning Exhibition Center ⊳ **37** Intriguing center showing the Shanghai of the future.

Tianzifang ⊳ **28** Fascinating warren of alleyways, shikumen housing, small shops and studios.

Soong Qing-ling's Residence ⊳ **27** The home of Sun Yat-sen's widow is an attractive European villa dating from the 1920s.

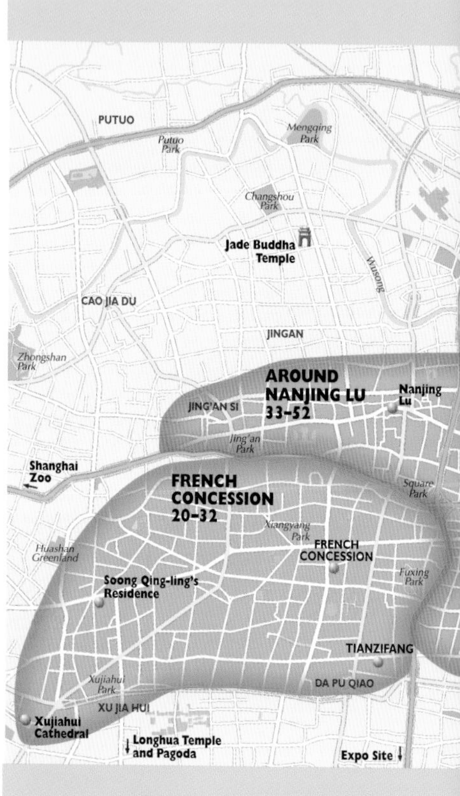

Shanghai Zoo ⊳ **104** Pandas, tigers and other creatures in one of the city's greenest parklands.

Shanghai Museum ⊳ **42–43** World-class modern museum dedicated to Chinese arts and crafts.

Pudong Skyscrapers ⊳ **94** The Manhattan of Shanghai is growing new high-rises every year.

These pages are a quick guide to the Top 25, which are described in more detail later. Here they are listed alphabetically, and the tinted background shows which area they are in.

Expo Site ▷ 100–101 The former world's fair site has a brace of intriguing art museums.

Fairmont Peace Hotel ▷ 62 Shanghai's greatest art-deco monument is now a swanky hotel.

French Concession and Markets ▷ 24–25 Leafy neighborhood with great shopping, as well as sights.

Huangpu Riverboat Tour ▷ 60–61 Get a different perspective of the city from the water.

Huxinting Tea House ▷ 70–71 The familiar building from blue Willow Pattern china.

Jade Buddha Temple ▷ 102–103 Shanghai's most famous temple, with two jade Buddhas.

Longhua Temple and Pagoda ▷ 26 Elegantly restored active temple complex.

Lu Xun Park ▷ 86–87 Park dedicated to modernist writer Lu Xun.

Nanjing Lu ▷ 36 Shanghai's most famous shopping street, partly pedestrianized.

Old Town ▷ 72–73 Enclave packed with traditional tenement houses and street markets.

People's Square ▷ 40–41 The bustling heart of Shanghai, ringed by modern towers.

People's Park ▷ 38–39 Pleasant, tranquil space with museums and a pond, right in the heart of the city.

Oriental Pearl Tower ▷ 92–93 This tower has long symbolized Pudong in east Shanghai.

Shopping

If mainland China has a shopping heart, it has to be Shanghai. From busy clothing markets and stylish boutiques to upscale department stores and brand new mega-malls, the city finds itself permanently at the forefront of the nation's consumer drive.

Nanjing Lu

Nanjing Lu is mainland China's most famous shopping street. While it is particularly touristy in parts, its western section, toward Jing'an Temple, has more style and a larger range of up-to-the-minute department stores. Much of the eastern end of Nanjing Lu has been transformed into a pedestrians-only precinct, which has made shopping there convenient, but this also draws in crowds of out-of-town sightseers. Nanjing Lu is no longer the unchallenged colossus it once was, however, and it has to work increasingly hard to hold its own against other shopping areas.

Other Major Streets

Huaihai Zhonglu, in the French Concession, is Nanjing Lu's stylish competitor. North of central Huaihai Zhonglu are several small roads—Changle Lu and Xinle Lu among them—lined with fashionable boutiques for clothes and shoes. Tianzifang (▷ 28) is a charming warren of alleys devoted to small artist studios, jewelry shops, clothing stores and cafés. Xintiandi (▷ 44) has a high-profile retail component.

SHOPPING IN PUDONG

More major shopping areas are opening up all the time. The most important of these is on the Pudong side of the Huangpu River. The area is rather hit and miss, with a preponderance of high-end malls and glittering hotel arcades, so the feeling is of a rather purpose-built and charmless place. Beyond the malls, Pudong is also home to the subterranean Yatai Xinyang Fashion and Gift Market. It is one of Shanghai's best market experiences and an excellent jaunt if you love full-on haggling, but you'll have to fend the vendors off!

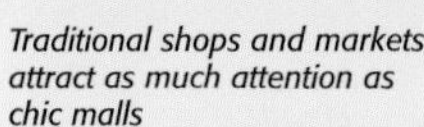

Traditional shops and markets attract as much attention as chic malls

Shop for exotic or everyday items in a rapidly growing range of outlets

The Old Town's Yuyuan area (▷ panel, below) is great for souvenirs and collectibles. Pudong is home to some monster-malls, but is uninspiring for shopping, although this could change in the future (▷ 10, panel). The 50 Moganshan Road Art District (▷ 48) also has a number of trendy shops. More staid Fuzhou Lu is noted for its culturally oriented shops, selling antiques, old books and fine art items.

Department Stores

In addition to individual shops and boutiques, Nanjing Lu hosts several of Shanghai's most notable department stores, shopping malls and supermarkets, among them the New World department store (▷ 48), Shanghai Number One department store and the Plaza 66 mall (▷ 48). Streets running off Nanjing Lu add to its allure, with superior shopping malls like Raffles City (▷ 49). Huaihai Zhonglu also has several top department stores, including Hong Kong Plaza, Times Square and the Parkson Department Store, and Hongkou weighs in with the new Hongkou Plaza development (▷ 87).

Markets

Shanghai's many street markets are both a resource for reasonably priced goods, and even some bargains, and an attraction in their own right, filled with local atmosphere. Some of the best are in the Old Town.

YUYUAN AREA

Although the rather touristy area in and around Yuyuan in the Old Town cannot be considered a shopper's paradise in the way that some of the main shopping streets are, in some respects it is more popular with visitors. This is where you can find no end of antiques, arts and crafts, traditional medicines, souvenirs, and all kinds of minor commodities. Most of these go for reasonable prices—but in most cases only after the purchaser has bargained with great tenacity. The crowds that gather here to peruse, bargain and buy are, if anything, more densely packed than those elsewhere.

Shopping by Theme

Whether you're looking for a department store, a quirky boutique, or something in between, you'll find it all in Shanghai. On this page shops are listed by theme. For a more detailed write-up, see the individual listings in Shanghai by Area.

Art Galleries

50 Moganshan Road Art District (▷ 48)
Rockbund Art Museum (▷ 63)

Books

Garden Books (▷ 31)
Shanghai Foreign Language Bookstore (▷ 49)
Shanghai Museum Shop (▷ 49)

Department Stores and Malls

1933 (▷ 87)
Chia Tai Department Store (▷ 96)
City Plaza (▷ 48)
Hongkou Plaza (▷ 87)
Isetan (▷ 48)
New World (▷ 48)
Plaza 66 (▷ 48–49)
Raffles City (▷ 49)
Shanghai Centre (▷ 45)
Wal-Mart Supercenter (▷ 96)
Yatai Xinyang Fashion and Gift Market (▷ 96)

Fashion

City Plaza (▷ 48)
New World (▷ 48)
Shanghai Fashion Store (▷ 49)

Food and Drink

City Shop (▷ 48)
Huangshan Tea Company (▷ 31)
Old Shanghai Tea House (▷ 79)
Shanghai No. 1 Food Store (▷ 49)
Shao Wan Sheng (▷ 49)

Markets

Fuyou Market (▷ 76)
Huabao Building Antiques Market (▷ 78)
Shanghai Old Street (▷ 78)
Shiliupu Fabric Market (▷ 78)
South Bund Fabric Market (▷ 78)

Souvenirs

Blue Shanghai White (▷ 65)
Guo Chun Xiang Curiosity Shop (▷ 87)
Madame Mao's Dowry (▷ 31)
Pilingpalang (▷ 48)
Shanghai Jingdezhen Porcelain Artware Store (▷ 49)
Shanghai Museum Shop (▷ 49)
Silk King (▷ 65)
Silk World (▷ 78)
Yuyuan Bazaar (▷ 76)

Traditional Shops

Chinese Printed Blue Nankeen Exhibition Hall (▷ 31)
Duoyunxuan Art Studio (▷ 48)
Shanghai Jingdezhen Porcelain Artware Store (▷ 49)
Suzhou Cobblers (▷ 65)

Shanghai by Night

Shanghai lights up after dark with modern pubs, clubs and cocktail bars as well as traditional Chinese opera

Nightlife options are expanding almost daily—and nightly—in China's most cutting-edge city, a place that lives hard and plays hard. Loaded with panache, charisma, cash and an insatiable appetite for music, drink and sophistication, Shanghai has entertainment in its DNA.

Traditional to Modern

As soon as darkness falls, the city lights up as jazz clubs, wine bars, clubs, pubs, cocktail bars and live music venues throw open their doors to well-dressed crowds. And there is a growing palette of highbrow entertainment to choose from, with offerings both traditional and modern, Chinese and international: The list includes classical music, opera, theater and dance, as well as spectacular and artistic acrobatics shows.

Quick Change

Keeping up with the rapid changes shaking up Shanghai's nightlife scene is a 24/7 job. Clubs, pubs and other venues open, fold or transform with astonishing rapidity. An old-timer is perhaps a cocktail bar with ten years on the clock but, even then, it may have moved twice or changed its name. What is certain is that you'll be spoiled for choice and, indeed, knowing where to start—or when to stop—can prove to be the biggest headache.

LISTINGS

Several English-language magazines give accessible information about what's on. *Time Out* has a monthly magazine that covers events, things to do, eating out, drinking, the arts and music scenes and more, with an associated website (timeoutshanghai.com) that has an online version of the magazine.

Also monthly, *That's Shanghai* does a similar job, with a website at thatsmags.com/shanghai.

With an online presence but no print edition, *Shanghaiist* (shanghaiist.com) and *Smart Shanghai* (smartshanghai.com) are also handy resources.

Where to Eat

Shanghai is naturally the optimum place in China to sample its namesake cooking, Shanghai cuisine, considered to be a version of the Huaiyang (also known as Yangzhou) cuisine of the lower Yangtze delta. Chefs working in these styles have, across hundreds if not thousands of years, added to a rich store of dishes, menus, ingredients and cooking methods.

Shanghai Cuisine

The city's indigenous cuisine has a number of distinctive characteristics. The "drunken" label attached to some classic dishes, for instance drunken chicken (*zuiji*) or drunken crabs (*zuixie*), arises because they are either marinated or cooked in alcohol such as rice wine. Vinegar, particularly the famed vinegar produced in nearby Zhejiang, is another popular ingredient. Sugar is often used as a sweetener, though since it is generally combined with vinegar, alcohol or soy sauce—or all three together—it creates a sweet-and-sour or savory taste. Since the city is so close to the sea, and because it stands on or near to the Huangpu and Yangtze rivers, sea and freshwater fish and crustaceans form a big part of the menu in city restaurants.

International Menus

As befits its status as China's premier international gateway city, Shanghai indulges in a full-on choice of international cuisine styles, along with niche eats, pop-up restaurants and the correct observance of food fashions.

CHINESE STYLES

The city is a rapidly growing melting pot of people from around China. Many have brought their own distinctive regional and even local cuisines with them. There is no shortage of restaurants, ranging from chic high-end places to on-street eateries, serving Cantonese, Sichuan, Pekingese and other major cuisines. You'll also find Tibetan, Mongolian, Xinjiang, Taiwanese, and even Hong Kong and Macanese (Macau) restaurants.

Shanghai's restaurants are bursting with Chinese, Asian and international flavors; Huxinting Tea House (right)

Where to Eat by Cuisine

There are plenty of places to eat to suit all tastes and budgets in Shanghai. On this page they are listed by cuisine. For a more detailed description of each venue, see Shanghai by Area.

Cafés
Baker & Spice (▷ 32)
Element Fresh (▷ 51)
Sumerian (▷ 52)

Chinese
Afanti Restaurant (▷ 87)
Din Tai Fung (▷ 51)
Dischui Dong (▷ 32)
Lost Heaven (▷ 32)
Pinchuan (▷ 52)

European
Commune Social (▷ 51)
Jean Georges (▷ 66)
M on the Bund (▷ 66)
Mr & Mrs Bund (▷ 66)

International
Ajisen (▷ 66)
Boxing Cat Brewery (▷ 32)
Grand Brasserie (▷ 66)
Jade on 36 (▷ 96)
On 56 (▷ 96)
Kathleen's 5 (▷ 52)
Rhumerie Bounty (▷ 32)
T8 (▷ 52)
Vue Bar (▷ 87)

Shanghainese
Bao Luo (▷ 32)
The Grape (▷ 32)
Lao Fandian (Shanghai Old Restaurant ▷ 79)
Lu Bo Lang (▷ 79)
Lynn (▷ 52)
Nan Xiang (▷ 79)
Shanghai Grandmother (▷ 66)

Street food
Wujiang Lu food street (▷ 51)

Teahouses
Huxinting Tea House (▷ 79)
Old Shanghai Tea House (▷ 79)

Vegetarian
Gongdelin (▷ 51)
Jade Buddha Temple restaurant (▷ 102)
Songyuelou (▷ 79)
Vegetarian Lifestyle (▷ 52)

Top Tips For...

These great suggestions will help you tailor your ideal visit to Shanghai, no matter how you choose to spend your time. Each sight or listing has a fuller write-up elsewhere in the book.

Clockwise from top left: Cool jewelry; the art deco Fairmont Peace Hotel; enjoy a cocktail at a smart bar or take in an

INTERNATIONAL SHOPPING

Head for Xintiandi (▷ 44) and its trendy boutique shopping in traditional streets.
Isetan (▷ 48) offers department-store class, Japanese style.
For Western eatables and other products, visit City Shop (▷ 48).
Browse through the warren of small shops and boutiques at Tianzifang (▷ 28).

TRADITIONAL SHOPPING

Shanghai Jingdezhen Porcelain Artware Store (▷ 49) sells fine ceramics from the famed Jingdezhen kilns southwest of Shanghai, in Jiangxi province.
Shop for hand-embroidered silk slippers at Suzhou Cobblers (▷ 65).
Pick up traditional blue-and-white Chinese clothing at the Chinese Printed Blue Nankeen Exhibition Hall (▷ 31).

LOCAL CUISINE

Shanghai Grandmother (▷ 66) serves terrific local favorites from its ever-popular address.
Bao Luo (▷ 32) provides tasty and authentic Shanghai food.
Singe your taste buds devouring spicy Hunan cuisine at the Dischui Dong (▷ 32).
Indulge in a modern take on Shanghai cuisine at the stylish Lynn restaurant (▷ 52).

PLEASING THE KIDS

Mickey Mouse and crew await at Shanghai Disneyland in Pudong (▷ 95).
Marvel at the high-altitude views from Shanghai Tower's observation deck (▷ 94).
Shanghai Maglev (▷ 116), the high-speed train system, is a must for speed-freaks.

acrobatics show; tuck into a tasty local dish; savor some traditional Chinese tea; shopping in Xintiandi

CHARACTER HOTELS

The Fairmont Peace Hotel (▷ 62, 112) is one of the outstanding colonial-era art deco buildings on the Bund.

Intercontinental Shanghai Ruijin (▷ 111) comprises 1920s red-brick villas in a stunning setting with balconies overlooking its walled Japanese garden.

Enjoy the period charms of Kevin's Old House (▷ 111), seasoned with delightful sensations of old Shanghai.

HOT AND COOL EXPERIENCES

Soak up the sights of Pudong's spectacular skyline from the rooftop Sir Elly's Terrace (▷ 65), the Bund's largest terrace.

At Bar Rouge (▷ 65) the well-prepared cocktails are followed by well-crafted DJ sounds.

Get into the groove with top international DJs on one of Shanghai's largest dance floors at Myst (▷ 50).

Glam Bar (▷ 65): The name says it all—it's a glamorous bar in a great position on the Bund.

ENTERTAINMENT

Cathay Theatre (▷ 31) offers the best Chinese and international cinema in a 1930s art deco gem of a building.

Shanghai Symphony Orchestra Hall (▷ 31) is the striking home of the Shanghai Symphony Orchestra.

Shanghai Conservatory of Music (▷ 31) is a wonderful venue for classical music, both Chinese and Western.

Shanghai Centre Theatre (▷ 50) is the place for enjoying mind-spinning acrobatics.

SAVING MONEY

The Metro (▷ 118) is fast and especially good value for long journeys.

Stay in Shanghai for 144 hours visa-free, as long as you are moving on to a third country (▷ 116).

Drinks can be extortionate, so use happy hour prices to lessen the sting.

LOOKING FOR A BARGAIN

Shanghai Grandmother (▷ 66) serves affordable and tasty home-style Shanghai cooking.

Ajisen (▷ 66) offers diners excellent bowls of spicy Japanese noodles, a photo menu and brisk service.

Shanghai Museum (▷ 42–43) is China's best museum and it's currently free to visit.

The Bund (▷ 58–59) is Shanghai's top sight and it won't cost you a penny.

THE SCENT OF SANCTITY

Longhua Temple and Pagoda (▷ 26) is Shanghai's most venerable Buddhist temple and dates back to the Song dynasty.

Xujiahui Cathedral (▷ 29) was founded by Jesuit priests, and is still a stronghold of the Chinese Catholic church.

Jade Buddha Temple (▷ 102–103) is Shanghai's best-known Buddhist Temple.

COLONIAL AIRS AND GRACES

Not everything in the French Concession (▷ 24–25) is French, but enough francophone architecture, parks and broad boulevards survive to give the idea of a certain prewar *je ne sais quoi*.

Soong Qing-ling's former residence (▷ 27), a 1920s European-style villa, was once home to the wife of the founder of modern China, Sun Yat-sen.

Wander up and down the Bund (▷ 58–59) to experience the strongest sensations of concession-era Shanghai.

Explore 1933 (▷ 87), a magnificent deco-era slaughterhouse in Hongkou, built by the British and site of splendid photo ops.

TAKING A TEA BREAK

Savor the ultimate Chinese tea experience at Huxinting Tea House (▷ 70–71).

Relax after a hard day's sightseeing at the tranquil Old Shanghai Tea House (▷ 79).

See re-creations of old-style teahouses at the Urban Planning Exhibition Center (▷ 37).

From top: Fuyou Market; Longhua Temple; an evocative wall painting in the French Concession; evening drinks

Shanghai by Area

龍華寺

French Concession

The stylish French Concession ranges from elegant art deco apartment blocks, dignified shikumen architecture and narrow lilong alleys to trendy boutiques, chic restaurants and tree-shaded streets reminiscent of La France.

Top 25

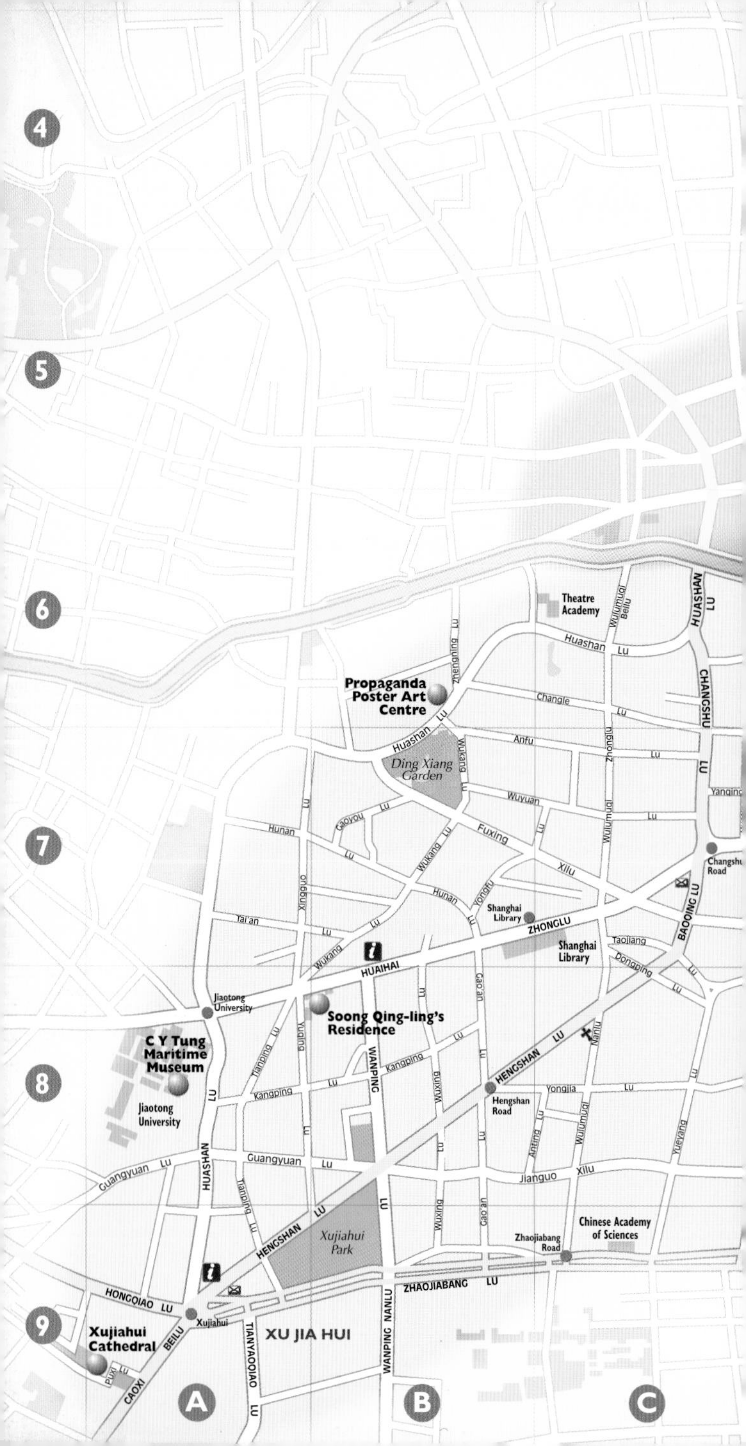
4
5
6
7
8
9
A
B
C
Propaganda Poster Art Centre
Soong Qing-ling's Residence
C Y Tung Maritime Museum
Xujiahui Cathedral
Theatre Academy
Ding Xiang Garden
Shanghai Library
Jiaotong University
Xujiahui Park
Chinese Academy of Sciences
XU JIA HUI
HUASHAN LU
CHANGSHU LU
BAOQING LU
HUAIHAI
ZHONGLU
HENGSHAN LU
WANPING NANLU
ZHAOJIABANG LU
HONGQIAO LU
CAOXI BEILU
TIANYAOQIAO LU
Huashan Lu
Changle Lu
Anfu Lu
Wuyuan Lu
Fuxing Xilu
Hunan Lu
Gaoyou Lu
Wukang Lu
Tai'an Lu
Taojiang
Dongping Lu
Yongfu
Kangping Lu
Guangyuan Lu
Jianguo Xilu
Yongjia Lu
Tianping Lu
Xingguo
Zhenning Lu
Wulumuqi Beilu
Wulumuqi
Zhonglu
Gao'an Lu
Wuxing Lu
Anting Lu
Yueyang
Yuqing
Nanlu
Yanging
Puxi Lu
Jiaotong University
Changshu Road
Hengshan Road
Zhaojiabang Road
Xujiahui

French Concession

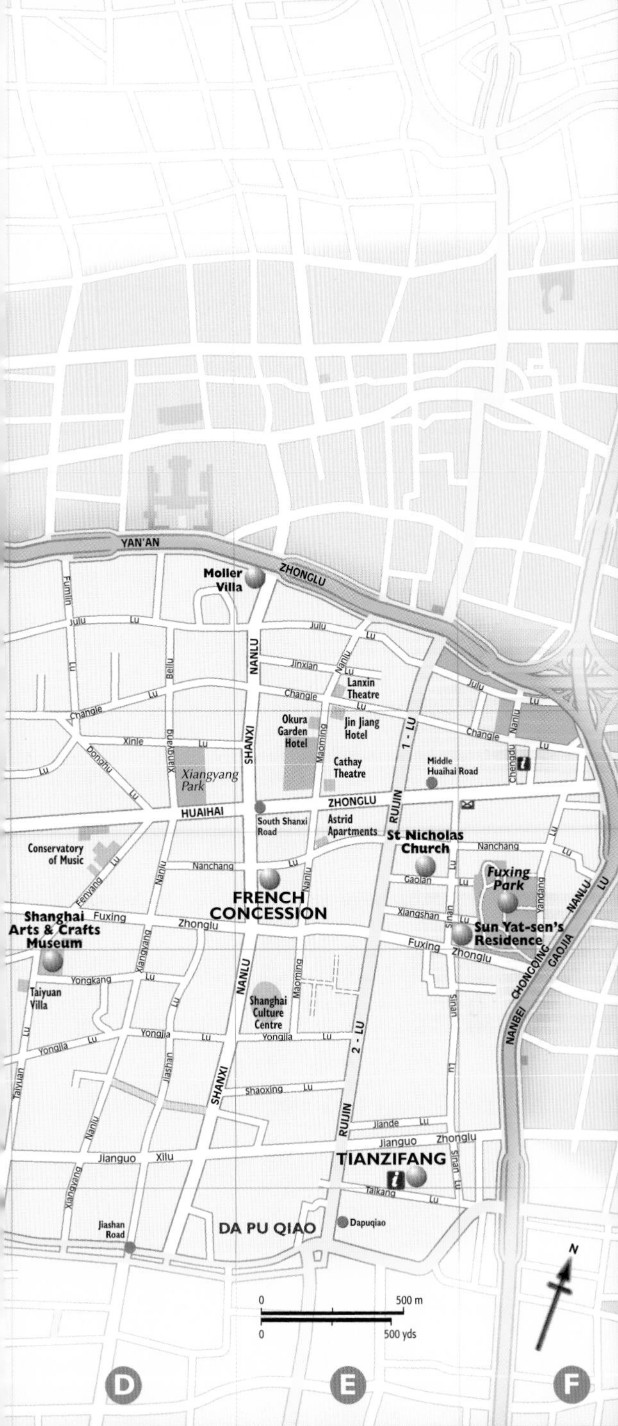

French Concession and Markets

TOP 25

HIGHLIGHTS

- Fascinating colonial-era architecture
- Excellent shopping
- Fine restaurants and bars
- Theaters and cinemas
- Small but welcome parks

TIP

- Huaihai Zhonglu, which slices laterally through the French Concession, runs for 3.5 miles (6km). Three Metro stations—Huangpi Road (S), Changshu Road and Shanxi Road (S)—are dotted along it.

Oozing style and sophistication, the French Concession—"Frenchtown"—is a blend of restaurants, discerning cafés, stylish boutiques, art deco architecture and European-style villas.

France Outre Mer The French Concession lay to the south of the original British Settlement, and to the west of the old Chinese town. Having grown to 4sq miles (10sq km), it refused the invitation to join the Americans and British in forming the International Settlement in 1863. The French Settlement had its own buses and trams, its own electricity and its own judicial system and traffic regulations—and it added spice to the steaming cosmopolitan brew that was Shanghai. Gangsters, revolutionaries, bon-vivants and refugees were attracted

Clockwise from left: Pedestrians on busy Huaihai Zhonglu; relaxing with tea and a good book; traditional cloth designs at the Chinese Printed Blue Nankeen Exhibition Hall (▷ 31); enjoying evening drinks outside

to the Concession and, by 1930, the French residents were outnumbered by Americans, Britons and Russians.

Touring the French Concession The heart of the old Concession was Avenue Joffre, today's Huaihai Zhonglu, which is as good a shopping street as the more famous Nanjing Lu (▷ 36). Tianzifang (▷ 28) is excellent for shopping and dining in an attractive shikumen environment. Art deco buildings are at every turn, from the Jinjiang Hotel to the Cathay Theatre, while other gems—St. Nicholas Church, the Intercontinental Shanghai Ruijin, the Moller Villa—dot the tree-lined streets. Another standout relic is the grandiose entrance to the former French club, Le Cercle Sportif Francais (now part of the Okura Garden Hotel Shanghai, ▷ 112).

THE BASICS

- C7–F7
- Around Huaihai Zhonglu
- Many excellent restaurants
- Shanxi Road (S)
- 10, 42, 911
- None

Longhua Temple and Pagoda

The gates to the temple (left); worshipers inside; a carved lion (right)

THE BASICS

- Off map at B9
- 2853 Longhua Lu
- 6457 6327
- Daily 7–4.30
- Vegetarian restaurant
- Metro line 11 to Longhua
- None
- Inexpensive

HIGHLIGHTS

- Handsome pagoda
- Active temple

TIP

- The best times to visit are at New Year or during one of the festivals: Birthday of the Queen of Heaven (Mar 23), Birthday of Sakyamuni Buddha (Apr 8), the Longhua Temple Fair (May Day and October National Vacation Weeks), when there are processions and music.

Meaning "Magnificence of the Dragon Temple", Longhua Temple is Shanghai's largest Buddhist temple complex. An active temple, the site is perhaps best known for its elegant pagoda, which rises opposite its main gate.

The Pagoda Unusually for Chinese pagodas that survive with their associated Buddhist temples, the stupa here rises up beyond the main temple grounds. The pagoda's foundations date from AD977 (Song dynasty), and although the pagoda has certainly been rebuilt many times since then, it retains the architectural features of the Song period. Seven floors and 134ft (41m) high, the pagoda is octagonal and made of wood and brick, with "flying" eaves of gray tile; unfortunately, it cannot be climbed. It stands on the site of another pagoda, thought to have been built during the period known as the Three Kingdoms (AD238–251).

The Temple According to legend, the Longhua Temple was founded during the Three Kingdoms period by the king of Wu and Kang Monk Hui, the son of an eminent minister. It is more likely that its earliest construction was during the Five Dynasties period (AD923–979). The current buildings date from the end of the 19th century, during the final (Qing) dynasty. The main hall of the temple contains a large effigy of Sakyamuni, while the temple grounds are noted for their peach blossom in spring.

The front garden (left); a limousine presented to Soong Qing-ling (right)

Soong Qing-Ling's Residence

The villa of Soong Qing-ling, widow of Sun Yat-sen, the father of Republican China, paints a charming portrait of a vanished Shanghai era. A visit here gives glimpses of how the wealthy lived during a vital period in China's modern history.

Soong Qing-ling Born in Shanghai in 1893 to a family whose business was Bible printing, Soong Qing-ling was introduced to Sun Yat-sen through her father's connections with secret societies dedicated to the fall of the emperor. In 1913, on her way home from the US, where she was educated, she met Sun in Japan rallying support for the restoration of the republic he had founded in 1911. She became his secretary and married him in 1915. After Sun's death she became disenchanted with his successor, Chiang Kai Shek, and went to Moscow, returning to help with the anti-Japanese war effort. After the revolution she became a useful symbol for China until her death in 1981.

The Residence Soong Qing-ling's home in Shanghai from 1948 to 1963, in the heart of the French Concession, dates from the 1920s. The house, a European-style villa with a delightful garden, has been maintained as it was when she lived here. As befits the home of a representative of the people, it is furnished fairly simply, although there is an interesting collection of gifts from a number of eminent visitors, including a carpet from Mao, and a work in bamboo from Kim Il Sung of North Korea.

THE BASICS

shsoong-chingling.com
- B8
- 1843 Huaihai Zhonglu
- 6474 7183
- Daily 9–4.30
- Jiaotong University
- None
- Inexpensive

HIGHLIGHTS

- Lovely prewar villa with period furnishings
- Well-tended European-style garden

Tianzifang

Browsing the shops and cafés in Tianzifang's alleys

THE BASICS

- E8
- Lane 210, Taikang Lu
- Restaurants and cafés
- Dapuqiao
- None

HIGHLIGHTS

- Shikumen architecture
- Shopping
- Taking a coffee break

TIP

- There's plenty to see so allow several hours to explore Tianzifang's charming alleyways to soak up their old-world atmosphere.

Admire Shanghai's alleyway shikumen architecture while shopping at some of the city's most creative clothes shops and sipping coffee at trendy cafés. This small tangle of lanes is a great alternative to Shanghai's mega-malls.

Shikumen Style Like Beijing's siheyuan courtyard architecture, Shanghai's shikumen residences are motifs of the city. A marriage of 19th-century British terrace housing and traditional Chinese courtyards, shikumen buildings—tucked away in rows down alleys called lilong—are low-rise, with two or three floors, and fronted with an often elaborately carved stone lintel, lending the name shikumen (stone-surrounded gate). In Tianzifang (also called Taikang Lu Art Street), many of these old shikumen residences are now shops.

A Welcome Escape Not as well known as Xintiandi (▷ 44), Tianzifang has a manageable charm that makes a visit a more relaxing experience. Alleys branch off from the main lanes, leading to courtyards and further alleys with boutiques, jewelry shops, art galleries, cafés and restaurants. Explore quaint passageways to find hidden delights, from photographic galleries of daily life in China to personal tailors; and studios producing hand-crafted wares. Lane 210 has some of the most interesting establishments, but you can find others along Lanes 248 and 274. Watch the world go by at Boho Café Kommune (No. 7, Lane 210).

The cathedral's ornate ceiling (left) and altar (right)

TOP 25 Xujiahui Cathedral

In a country of Buddhist, Confucian and Taoist traditions that is now officially atheist, it is surprising to see the twin towers of a redbrick neo-Gothic cathedral poking into the sky in the shadow of gleaming skyscrapers.

The Jesuits The influence of Jesuit missionaries was felt in Shanghai from as early as the 16th century. An early convert was one Xu Guangqi, a native of Xujiahui, or "Xu Family Village," which at that time was well outside the original town of Shanghai. Xu, an official in the Imperial library, was baptized Paul. He later bequeathed family land to the Jesuits, where an observatory and cathedral would eventually be constructed. Following persecution of the converts, the first church here became a temple to the god of war; after the Treaty of Nanking (1842), the land was given to the French, and in 1848 a Jesuit settlement was established.

The Cathedral The current cathedral of St. Ignatius was built in 1906 with two 165ft (50m) spires and capacity for a congregation of 2,500. The interior includes a number of decorative idiosyncracies that indicate Buddhist influence—melons appear on the nave columns, along with stylized bats (a Chinese symbol of happiness), in the windows. Outside, gargoyles fringe the roof and a holy grotto has been built in the garden. Severely damaged during the Cultural Revolution, the cathedral is now a busy place of worship.

THE BASICS

- A9
- 158 Puxi Lu
- 6438 4632
- Mon–Sat 9–11, 1–4
- Xujiahui
- 3, 42, 50
- None
- Free
- Services Mon–Fri 6am, 7am; Sat 6am, 7am, 6pm; Sun 6am, 7.30am, 10am, 6pm

HIGHLIGHTS

- European neo-Gothic among the skyscrapers
- Catholic-style detailing

TIP

- Pop into the nearby Bibliotheca Zi-Ka-Wei (80 Caoxi Beilu) and visit the reading room upstairs; the awe-inspiring Jesuit library itself can only be visited by application.

More to See

C.Y. TUNG MARITIME MUSEUM

Wander around nearby historic Jiaotong University before visiting this museum, which is dedicated to Chinese maritime history.

A8 Jiaotong University 6293 2403 Tue–Sun 9–5 Xujiahui Free

FUXING PARK

A private garden converted in 1908 into a Parisian-style park and pleasantly shaded by Wutong trees, Fuxing Park is a delicious spot for a relaxing stroll.

F7 Fuxing Zhonglu Daily Restaurants Xintiandi 24, 36, 780, 781 None Free

MOLLER VILLA

mollervilla.com

Completed in 1936 and now a landmark hotel, this rather fantastical concoction of Gothic towers and spires was home to a Scandinavian shipping magnate.

Wooden staircase inside the Moller Villa

E6 30 Shaanxi Nanlu 6247 8881 Shanxi Road (S) 1, 42, 48, 71, 127

PROPAGANDA POSTER ART CENTRE

shanghaipropagandaart.com

This gallery exhibits a fine collection of political propaganda posters from the Mao era. It's a quirky diversion and a reminder of China's recent radicalism.

B6 Room B-OC, President Mansion, 868 Huashan Lu 6211 1845 Daily 10–5 Shanghai Library 48, 93, 113, 328 Moderate

ST. NICHOLAS CHURCH

Just west of Fuxing Park, this 1930s Russian Orthodox Church, now empty, is an attractive feature of Gaolan Lu.

E7 16 Gaolan Lu Huangpi Road (S)

SHANGHAI ARTS & CRAFTS MUSEUM

shgmb.com

This museum of traditional Chinese arts and crafts is in an elegant mansion with a beautiful garden.

D8 79 Fenyang Lu 6431 4074 Daily 9–5 Changshu Road 42 None Inexpensive

SUN YAT-SEN'S RESIDENCE

sh-sunyat-sen.org

The house of the father of Republican China has been kept as it supposedly was during his life, simply furnished in a mix of Western and Chinese styles.

F7 7 Xiangshan Lu 5306 3361 Daily 9–4.30 Shanxi Road (S) 2, 17, 24, 36, 42 Inexpensive

Shopping

CHINESE PRINTED BLUE NANKEEN EXHIBITION HALL

Also serving as a museum, this lovely exhibition hall displays and sells a gorgeous variety of blue and white fabrics. The simple but endlessly colorful designs are handmade and can be excellent gifts.

D7 No. 24, Lane 637, Changle Lu 5403 7947 Daily 9–5 Changshu Road

GARDEN BOOKS

gardenbooks.cn

Doubling as an ice-cream parlor, Garden Books has long been a literary mainstay of the French Concession, with a solid selection of books about Shanghai and China and a strong selection of novels.

E6 325 Changle Lu 5404 8728 Daily 10–10 Shanxi Road (S)

HUANGSHAN TEA COMPANY

This is the place to choose your favorite tea leaves from a vast selection of options from across the country, and to buy gorgeous ceramics and traditional hand-crafted clay Yixing teapots.

F7 605 Huaihai Zhonglu 5306 2258 Daily 9am–10pm Huangpi Road (S) 42, 911

MADAME MAO'S DOWRY

madamemaosdowry.com

This creative and eye-catching shop is always worth a browse, with its Cultural Revolution posters and cards, Mao statuettes, furniture, antiques, clothes, ceramics, art pieces and jewelry. Pieces are by local designers and artists, and selected for both their utility and beauty.

D6 207 Fumin Lu 5403 3551 Daily 10–7 Jing'an Temple

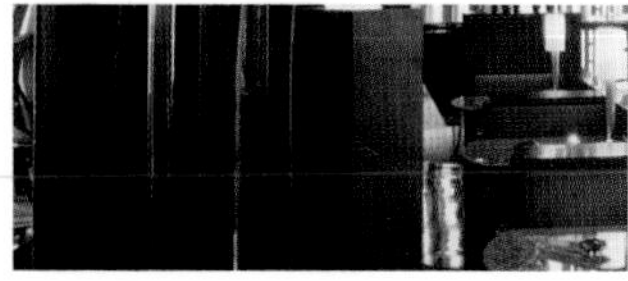

Entertainment and Nightlife

CATHAY THEATRE

guotaifilm.com

One of the most famous historic cinemas in town, this lovely restored 1930s theater is worth stopping by for its lovely art deco lines; it also shows Chinese and international films.

E7 870 Huaihai Zhonglu 5404 0415/5404 2095 Shanxi Road (S) 41

SHANGHAI CONSERVATORY OF MUSIC

Founded in 1927, and with many famous alumni, this conservatory has regular performances of classical Chinese and Western music most weekend evenings at 7.30pm.

D7 20 Fenyang Lu 6431 1792 Shanxi Road (S)

SHANGHAI SYMPHONY ORCHESTRA HALL

shsymphony.com

This striking concert hall is home to the Shanghai Symphony Orchestra and hosts leading overseas orchestras and well-known musicians, as well as smaller chamber groups, quartets and singers. It comprises a 1,200-seat main auditorium as well as a 400-seat chamber. Tickets tend to be reasonably priced and often sell out.

C7 1380 Fuxing Zhonglu 2426 6162 Changshu Road 42

Where to Eat

PRICES

Prices are approximate, based on a 3-course meal for one person.

$$$ more than 250RMB
$$ 100–250RMB
$ under 100RMB

BAKER & SPICE ($)

bakerandspice.com.cn

All you could want from a café: neat and appealing with excellent, wholesome food and chirpy staff. Tucked away down Anfu Lu, this is a good spot for breakfast, coffee, a sandwich or a delicious pastry; take a seat and watch the world go by.

B7 195 Anfu Lu 6234 0680 Daily 6am–10pm Changshu Road

BAO LUO ($)

baoluojiulou.com

Inviting Bao Luo is a longstanding French Concession mainstay with a loyal following, serving up some fantastically popular traditional Shanghai cuisine.

D6 271 Fumin Lu 6279 2827 Daily 11.30–3.30, 5pm–3am Changshu Road

BOXING CAT BREWERY ($$)

boxingcatbrewery.com

This popular venue brews European-style ales, lagers and American craft beers, while the food is spicy Southern US cuisine. Portions are big, so bring an appetite.

C7 82 Fuxing Xilu 6431 2091 Mon–Thu 5pm–2am, Fri 3pm–2am, Sat–Sun 10am–2am Shanghai Library

DISCHUI DONG ($)

One of Shanghai's most popular restaurants, this upstairs rustic-style eatery offers delectably spicy dishes from the central-southern province of Hunan, with staff dressed as peasants. If you love hot food, you'll adore this place.

E6 2nd floor, 56 Maoming Nanlu 6253 2689 Daily 11am–1am Shanxi Road (S)

THE GRAPE ($$)

Next to the Russian Orthodox Church on Xinle Lu, The Grape is an old French Concession favorite; service is friendly and the Shanghai and Yangzhou cuisine dependably good.

D7 55 Xinle Lu 5404 0486 Daily 11am–midnight 45 Shanxi Road (S)

LOST HEAVEN ($$)

lostheaven.com.cn

With another branch near the Bund, this very popular and atmospheric restaurant specializes in the southwestern cuisine of distant Yunnan province.

B7 38 Gaoyou Lu 6433 5126 Daily 11.30–1, 5.30–10.30 Hengshan Road

RHUMERIE BOUNTY ($)

bountybar.cn

Pizzas, calzone and meat skewers is about as exciting as the food gets here, but who cares when you're getting shipwrecked in this pirate-themed bar with more rums than you can shake a hook at.

B7 47 Yongfu Lu 6271 1406 Daily 6pm til late Changshu Road

EXPENSIVE OPTIONS

Always check the cost of dishes that do not have a price on them on the menu. Seasonal dishes, particularly those involving seafoods, can be expensive, even on an otherwise inexpensive menu.

Around Nanjing Lu

The busy shopping strip of Nanjing Lu feeds into the expanses of People's Park and People's Square, along with fascinating museums, skyscrapers and cultural showpieces.

Top 25

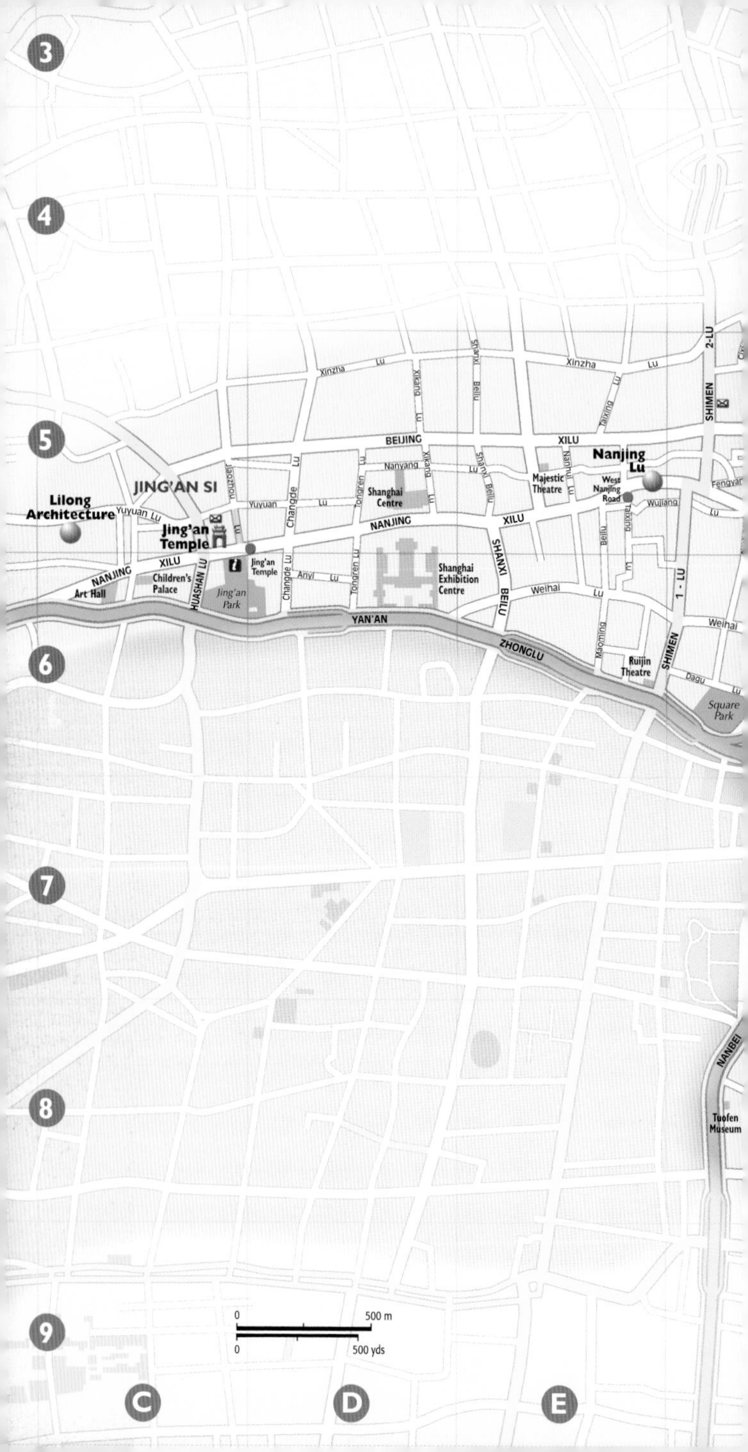

3
4
5
6
7
8
9
C
D
E
Xinzha
Lu
Xikang
Lu
Shanxi
Beilu
Taixing
Lu
2-LU
SHIMEN
BEIJING
XILU
Nanjing
Lu
JING'AN SI
Jiaozhou
Lu
Changde
Lu
Nanyang
Lu
Tongren
Lu
Shanghai
Centre
Majestic
Theatre
Nanhui
West
Nanjing
Road
Wujiang
Fengyang
Lilong
Architecture
Yuyuan Lu
Yuyuan
Lu
Jing'an
Temple
NANJING
XILU
SHANXI
BEILU
Jing'an
Temple
Anyi
Lu
Shanghai
Exhibition
Centre
Beilu
Taixing
Lu
1 - LU
NANJING
XILU
Children's
Palace
HUASHAN LU
Art Hall
Jing'an
Park
Changde Lu
Tongren Lu
Weihai
Lu
Weihai
YAN'AN
ZHONGLU
Maoming
Ruijin
Theatre
SHIMEN
Dagu
Lu
Square
Park
NANBEI
Tuofen
Museum
0
500 m
0
500 yds

Around Nanjing Lu

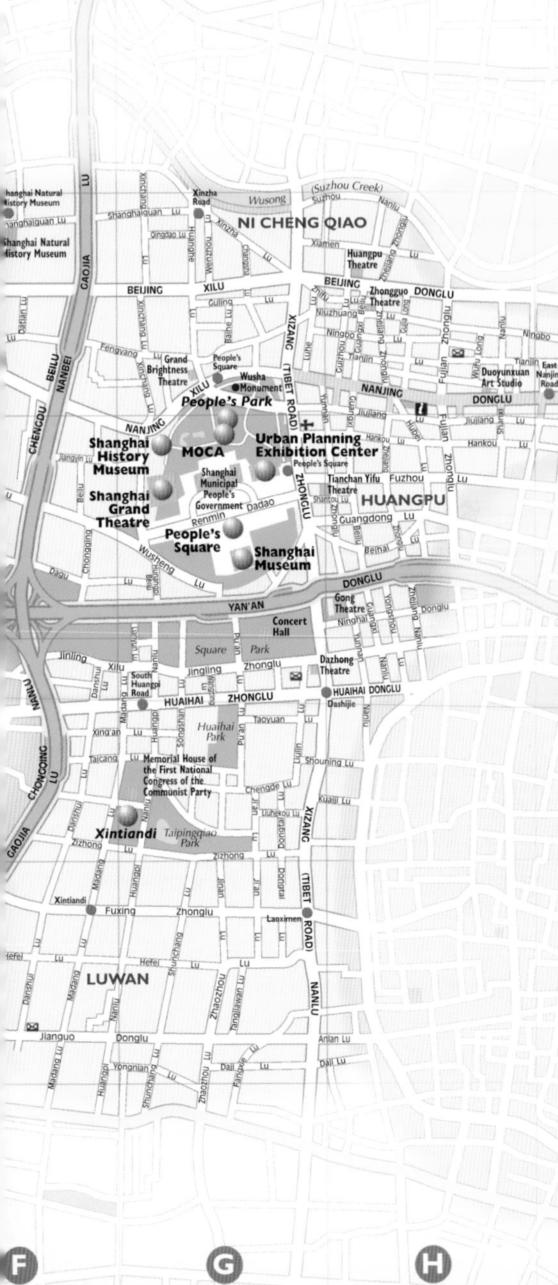

Nanjing Lu

TOP 25

Neon lights (left); distinctive skyscrapers line the road (right)

THE BASICS

C6–J5
Many excellent restaurants
Nanjing Road (E), People's Square, Nanjing Road (W), Jing'an Temple
20, 37
None

HIGHLIGHTS

- Heart of workaday Shanghai
- Excellent shopping
- Period architecture

TIP

- Nanjing Donglu can be noisy, with huge numbers of shoppers and tourists. If you want to evade the crowds and speed along the pedestrianized length of Nanjing Donglu, jump aboard one of the fun tourist "trains" that travel from the People's Square end to Henan Zhonglu. Tickets are inexpensive and trains leave regularly.

Starting at the Bund's Peace Hotel, storming through People's Square, and taking shoppers all the way west to the Jing'an Temple, Nanjing Road is Shanghai's most famous thoroughfare.

The Past Originally called Park Lane, linking the Bund to the racecourse in today's People's Park, the street was renamed Nanjing Road (Nanjing Lu) in 1862. As Shanghai grew, so did this street, snaking through the heart of the International Settlement to become, at its western end, the Bubbling Well Road (now Nanjing Xilu), named for a well near the Jing'an Temple.

Today Although rivaled by Huaihai Zhonglu for shopping, Nanjing Lu remains Shanghai's main thoroughfare, bordered in the east by the Bund and the Huangpu River. Nanjing Donglu (East Nanjing Road) is liveliest, especially the pedestrians-only strip between Henan Zhonglu and Xizang Zhonglu. Along Nanjing Donglu, look for art deco buildings, including the Peace Hotel (▷ 62). Other historic buildings include the Shanghai No. 1 Department Store and the former Shanghai Sincere Department Store, now the East Asia Hotel (▷ 109). Where Nanjing Donglu meets Nanjing Xilu (Nanjing Road West) is the old racecourse grandstand, once home to the Shanghai Art Museum, its collection now in the China Art Museum and Power Station of Art at the Expo Site (▷ 100–101), and the Park Hotel (▷ 109), once the tallest building outside the Americas.

Exterior of the center (left); scale model of the city (right)

TOP 25

Urban Planning Exhibition Center

This fascinating museum (Chengshi Guihua Zhanshiguan), on the eastern end of People's Square, propels visitors into the future by showing them what the city might look like in years to come.

What's in a Name? They could easily have given this museum a more appealing name, but don't judge it on this basis alone. Begin your odyssey on the mezzanine floor, where a 20-minute film takes you on a whistle-stop tour of 100 years of Shanghai history.

City Plans Prepare to be bowled over by the star attraction, a scale model of the city as it is planned to look in the future, so detailed that it takes up the entire third floor. The high-tech displays on the fourth floor turn the spotlight on mammoth construction projects like the Yangshan deep-water port and the Expo Site (▷ 100–101).

Relentless Change One rather sad exhibit is of older areas that are slated for demolition, to be replaced by modern apartments and offices. It may not be considered a loss by their current residents, whose wish for more comfortable accommodations will be fulfilled. Yet parts of town that might be worth saving and refurbishing will disappear, too, and there seems to be nothing to stop the development of so many parts of old Shanghai. In partial compensation, there are working re-creations of old shops and teahouses in the museum basement.

THE BASICS

supec.org
G6
100 Renmin Dadao
6372 2077
Tue–Thu 9–5, Fri–Sun 9–6 (last ticket one hour before closing). Closed Mon
Museum café
People's Square
46, 71, 123, 574
Moderate
Good

HIGHLIGHTS

- Scale model of Shanghai's future vision
- Top-floor café

TIP

- Take an opera glass or a small pair of binoculars for close-up views of the beautifully detailed scale model of Shanghai-to-be.

People's Park

TOP 25

HIGHLIGHTS

- Shanghai Museum of Contemporary Art
- People-watching
- Unhurried park tempo
- Lotus flowers in summer

TIP

- Greet the dawn in the park with enthusiasts who rise early for a tai chi lesson.

People's Park (Renmin Gongyuan) has evolved from a former British racecourse. A much-needed enclave of greenery and tranquility, the park is an escape from the crowds of People's Square.

Park Life Many visitors overlook the park, but it is lovely to have a stroll among its flower beds and manicured lawns. Be sure to visit the Shanghai Museum of Contemporary Art (▷ 45), perhaps the chief attraction. Alongside the pond is Barbarossa (▷ 50), a popular Moroccan-style terrace bar and restaurant. The park attracts office workers at lunchtime and in summer any tree-shaded bench is much in demand. Summer is also the season to catch the gorgeous pink lotuses that flower in the waters of the main pond.

Clockwise from left: Barbarossa restaurant in People's Park; view of Radisson Blu Hotel Shanghai New World from the park; a tranquil walk among the trees

Gentle Pursuits The racecourse had existed from 1862 and drew gamblers from around China, but it did not long survive the Communist takeover in 1949. Today, you'll see tai chi practitioners, stylized sword-fighters and kite flyers in the park's open spaces and on the adjoining People's Square (▷ 40). Groups of retired Chinese play mahjong and chess, brush up on their ballroom dancing and English (native speakers out for a stroll are popular "victims" for the latter), and engage in match-making for their grandchildren, who are far too busy climbing the corporate ladder and having fun to find time for mere matrimony. Other parts of the park have narrow paths and fairly dense clusters of trees and plants organized into a rigorously formal, landscaped setting.

THE BASICS

- G5–6
- Nanjing Xilu
- Daily 6–6
- People's Square
- 46, 71, 123, 574
- Free

People's Square

TOP 25

HIGHLIGHTS

- Shanghai Museum
- Renmin Park
- Shanghai Grand Theatre

TIP

- For long, long views over the city, take the elevator to the lobby of the J.W. Marriott Hotel, in dazzling Tomorrow Square, or slowly revolve while dining within Epicure on 45, at the summit of the Radisson Blu Hotel Shanghai New World.

If Shanghai's magnificent sprawl has a focal point, this is it. Many of the city's top attractions cluster here, among the swell of museum-goers, shoppers, white-collar workers and out-of-towners.

Bustling Hub Redesigned in the 1990s, People's Square—a popular name for city squares in China—is the equivalent of Beijing's Tiananmen Square, but far more accessible. As Shanghai's largest Metro interchange, the square and its environs are constantly flooded with people, crossing over to Nanjing Donglu, doing exercises, flying kites or taking a break.

Seeing the Sights The best way to negotiate People's Square (Renmin Guangchang) is to take the Metro exit to Renmin Dadao (People's

From left: The square is busy at all times of day; the top floors of the Radisson Blu Hotel Shanghai New World, north of the square

Avenue), which divides the square in half. All places of interest, except the standout Shanghai Museum (▷ 42), are on the north side. Following the avenue east to west takes you past the Urban Planning Exhibition Center (▷ 37) to the Shanghai Grand Theatre (▷ 45), north of which is the distinctive clock tower of the former Shanghai Art Museum, and the entrance to People's Park (▷ 38) beyond. Overlooking the square are some astronomically tall buildings, including Tomorrow Square, Brilliance Shimao International Plaza and the Radisson Blu Hotel Shanghai New World (▷ 111). Unlike Tiananmen Square, People's Square very much belongs to the people, who fill it with their own hobbies and pastimes, from ballroom dancing to pigeon-feeding, parasol-toting and people-watching.

THE BASICS

- G6
- People's Square
- Restaurants and cafés
- People's Square
- 46, 71, 123, 574
- Good

Shanghai Museum

TOP 25

HIGHLIGHTS

- Paintings and ceramics
- Bronzes and sculpture
- Excellent presentation

TIPS

- The audio tour is a very good investment, guiding you through the museum's many highlights.
- Try to get here early as the museum limits admissions to 8,000 people daily.

The Shanghai Museum contains China's foremost collection of ceramics, bronzes, art, calligraphy and Buddhist statues. You'll need a whole day to do it justice, and you could easily find yourself coming back for more.

The Museum The exterior is an eye-catching design, with its square base and circular crown, from which emanate four archlike handles—the ensemble is supposed to represent a Han dynasty bronze mirror or an ancient bronze *ding* tripod (an ancient food vessel). Built in the very heart of the city in 1996 to house a collection of some 120,000 cultural relics, the museum has 11 galleries and three exhibition halls. Despite tough competition, it possibly still ranks as the nation's best museum.

Clockwise from left: The imposing entrance to the museum; Yi water vessel from 771BC; a wider view showing the circular upper level; Qing dynasty (17th–20th century) woman's embroidered velvet jacket; Sclpture Gallery; a painting of a woman with a sword

Exhibits The thematic layout and intelligent lighting display exhibits to their best advantage. The principal galleries—which you really should not miss—are dedicated to ceramics, ancient bronzes, ancient sculpture and paintings. The ceramics section in particular is stunning—a majestic sweep from early pottery fragments to the gorgeous imperial pieces of the Ming and Qing dynasties. The dark patina bronzes are similarly spectacular, displaying the elaborate animistic patterns and designs of pre-Buddhist China. The ancient Chinese sculptures are largely Buddhist in inspiration and subject, forming what is probably China's best collection outside of the nation's grottoes. Other galleries are devoted to ancient Chinese jade, Ming and Qing furniture, art from China's ethnic minorities and Chinese calligraphy.

THE BASICS

shanghaimuseum.net
G6
201 Renmin Dadao
6372 3500
Tue–Sun 9–5 (last entry 4pm)
Cafés on the premises
People's Square
Good
Free
Audio tours (moderate for foreigners)

Xintiandi

TOP 25

Shikumen Open House Museum (left); a restored street in the area (right)

THE BASICS

- G7
- Huangpi Nanlu
- Many options
- Huangpi Road (S)
- 42, 109
- Good
- Corner of Taicang Lu and Huangpi Nanlu

HIGHLIGHTS

- Shikumen (stone-frame) houses
- Taipingqiao Park
- Trendy restaurants and cafés
- Boutique stores

TIP

- Xintiandi is just the first part of a redevelopment project of the zone around Taipingqiao Park. It is interesting to peruse the district to see how the changes are progressing. Be sure to take time out for a stroll around the handsome park, which has a pond at its heart.

A heavily restored and rebuilt quadrant of shikumen architecture, Xintiandi is a stylish blend of trendy bars and cafés, celebrated restaurants, boutiques, galleries, museums and clubs.

Housing Project The distinctive shikumen housing developed in the 19th century, a fusion of Chinese courtyard architecture and British terrace housing. By the early 1900s styles had changed and the houses fell into disrepair. In the 1990s developers decided to preserve the architecture of one run-down 1930s residential shikumen area by changing the buildings' function to shops and restaurants—while preserving the exterior walls and tiles.

Private History The history of the area and the cultural significance of the buildings are explained in the informative Shikumen Open House Museum (north block, Xintiandi; daily 10.30–10.30), which also presents the daily life of a typical family living here in the 1930s. The rooms are crammed with everyday objects and personal effects—movie posters, typewriters, radios, scent bottles, toys. The *tingzijian*, or "staircase room," between the first and second floors was usually rented out because its north-facing aspect made it cold in winter and hot in summer. The pithily named Memorial House of the First National Congress of the Communist Party of China speaks for itself. The main exhibit is a waxwork diorama dramatizing the founding congress of the Chinese Communist Party.

More to See

JING'AN SI (JING'AN TEMPLE)
shjas.org
The western part of Nanjing Lu was known as Bubbling Well Road until 1949. Before that it was Jing'an Road, named for this temple, which is over 1,700 years old. It burned down in the 1970s and nothing remains of the original buildings today (it's a rebuild).
C5 1686 Nanjing Xilu Daily 7–5 Jing'an Temple 20, 37 None Inexpensive

SHANGHAI GRAND THEATRE
shgtheatre.com
China's first purpose-built opera house (1998) was designed by French architect Jean-Marie Charpentier. Performances include opera, classics and musicals.
G6 300 Renmin Dadao 6386 8686 People's Square

SHANGHAI LILONG ARCHITECTURE
If you stroll west for half a mile (1km) along Yuyuan Lu from the art-deco Paramount Ballroom toward Zhenning Lu, you'll pass several preserved 1930s lilong alleyways with their characteristic residences, unique to Shanghai.
C5

SHANGHAI HISTORY MUSEUM
This museum moved from Lujiazui in 2018 to the magnificent former Race Club Building on the edge of People's Park, a far superior location to the basement of the Oriental Pearl TV Tower.
G6 325 Nanjing Xilu Tue–Sun 9–5 People's Square None Free

SHANGHAI MUSEUM OF CONTEMPORARY ART (MOCA)
mocashanghai.org
A great addition to Shanghai's gallery selection, MOCA stages international exhibitions within a glass-walled and thoroughly modern exhibiting space.
G6 People's Park 6327 9900 Daily 10–6 People's Square Inexpensive

The Shanghai History Museum

Jing'an Si occupies a site used for temples for the last 1,700 years

蔡同德堂

Nanjing Lu and People's Square

Nanjing Lu may no longer be the only shopping street in Shanghai, but it remains Shanghai's—and perhaps China's—most famous road.

DISTANCE: 2 miles (3km) **ALLOW:** 1.5 hours (not including stops)

START

FAIRMONT PEACE HOTEL
(▷ 62) J5 Nanjing Road (E)

1 Rising up handsomely along this first section of Nanjing Donglu from the Fairmont Peace Hotel are periodic art deco buildings and, of course, plenty of shops to admire.

2 Walk westward from the Nanjing Road (E) Metro station at Henan Zhonglu along the street's most famous section, the pedestrians-only stretch to People's Square (but watch out for traffic there).

3 If you want to, jump on one of the small and inexpensive tourist "trains" that ferry passengers all the way along the pedestrianized length of Nanjing Donglu. You will pass numerous department stores, hotels and shops, including the Duoyunxuan Art Studio at No. 422 (▷ 48).

4 Pop into the Shanghai No. 1 Food Store (▷ 49), at No. 720, for every kind of Chinese snack.

5 Cross Xizang Zhonglu to Nanjing Xilu and turn south into People's Park (▷ 38) to visit the Shanghai Museum of Contemporary Art (▷ 45).

6 Exit the park and walk west, past the Shanghai History Museum (▷ 45), or take the elevator to the foyer of the J.W. Marriott, high up in Tomorrow Square. Walk south to the Shanghai Grand Theatre (▷ 45), then east to the Urban Planning Exhibition Center (▷ 37).

7 Cross Renmin Dadao to the Shanghai Museum (▷ 42–43), the city's premier museum.

END

PEOPLE'S SQUARE (▷ 40–41)
G6 People's Square

Shopping

50 MOGANSHAN ROAD ART DISTRICT

Near Suzhou Creek, these art galleries, shops and cafés can easily take up half a day of browsing and window-shopping. Look out for standout art galleries ShanghArt (shanghartgallery.com) and Island6 (island6.org).

Off map 50 Moganshan Road
Hours vary, but most galleries open 10–6; most close Mon Shanghai Railway Station

CITY PLAZA

jiu-guang.com

This high-end shopping center, also known as Jiu Guang, features top international brands including Tiffany, Armani, Estée Lauder and Barbour. It also has restaurants and a Japanese grocery store.

D5 1618 Nanjing Xilu 3217 4838
Daily 10–10 Jing'an Temple

CITY SHOP

cityshop.com.cn

Expats and visitors flock to this branch (one of 13 in town) of a supermarket chain for international delicatessen items, brand-name food and more.

D5 Shanghai Centre, 1376 Nanjing Xilu
400 811 1797 Daily 8am–10.30pm
Jing'an Temple

DUOYUNXUAN ART STUDIO

duoyunxuan.com.cn

Arranged over several floors, Duoyunxuan is the place to come for calligraphy supplies, as well as paintings, stationery, rubbings of ancient carvings and seals (you can get your own seal carved here too). You can also find a selection of antiques.

H5 422 Nanjing Donglu 6360 6475
Daily 9.30am–9.30pm Nanjing Road (E)

ISETAN

isetan.cn/sh

Tokyo-based department store selling all the world's latest wares, though concentrating on items from Japan.

D5 1376 Nanjing Xilu 6272 1111
Daily 10am–9.30pm Nanjing Road (E)
23, 112

NEW WORLD

newworldcoltd.com

From Adidas to Ermenegildo Zegna, by way of Cerruti 1881, Esprit, Lacoste, Swarovski and Versace, the New World is focused on known international brand names, and fits them all handily into its extensive floor space.

G5 2–68 Nanjing Xilu 6358 8888
Daily 10–10 People's Square

PILINGPALANG

Gift or souvenir shoppers must come to Pilingpalang for its eye-catching range of fun and brightly colored ceramics, laquer and cloisonné items, bursting with style, grace and good taste. Designs are a gorgeous blend of art deco and Chinese traditional form.

F5 Shop 116, 1376 West Nanjing Road
6219 5020 Daily 10–9.30 Jing'an Temple

PLAZA 66

plaza66.com

Arguably the pick of the malls lining Shanghai's main shopping street,

CLOISONNÉ

Bronze ornaments are covered in a network of copper strips and then filled with layers of enamel paint, before being fired and polished—this is cloisonné. Good pieces are hard to find, and the best tend to be found among the antiques.

Plaza 66 is the place to head if money is no object. More than 100 designer brands are here.
E5 1266 Nanjing Xilu 6279 0910
Daily 10–10 Nanjing Road (W)

RAFFLES CITY

This Singaporean-owned mall has won plaudits for being a well-designed and comfortable place to shop. It's especially good for casual clothes, with a good spread of popular chains. There's also a cinema and spa.
G6 268 Xizang Zhonglu 6340 3600
Daily 10–10 People's Square

SHANGHAI FASHION STORE

blszsd.com
Selling an extensive range of clothes at moderate prices, this store is in part of a venerable building that once housed one of Shanghai's original department stores. Head to the top for a great range of children's literature.
H5 660–690 Nanjing Donglu 6322 5445 ext123 Daily 9.30am–10pm
Nanjing Road (E)

SHANGHAI FOREIGN LANGUAGE BOOKSTORE

This place has a decent selection of books in English and other languages, and books covering China, its culture and language. It also sells stationery.
H6 390 Fuzhou Lu 2320 4994
Daily 10–6.30 Nanjing Road (E)
17, 49

SHANGHAI JINGDEZHEN PORCELAIN ARTWARE STORE

Porcelain and handicrafts, many of them from the kilns at Jingdezhen, in Jiangxi province. The emphasis is on traditional rather than cutting-edge porcelain styles; shipping can be arranged.
E5 1175 Nanjing Xilu 6253 0885
Daily 10–10 Nanjing Road (W) 20, 37

SHANGHAI MUSEUM SHOP

shanghaimuseum.net
In fact, there are three shops on the southern side of the museum, which specialize in books, antiques and antique reproductions. It's an excellent place to pick up gifts or souvenirs.
G6 201 Renmin Dadao 6372 3500
Daily 9.30–5 People's Square 23

SHANGHAI NO. 1 FOOD STORE

This large supermarket stocks mainly Chinese products but has a growing range of international brands. It's good for picnics or for when you don't want to eat out at a restaurant.
H5 720 Nanjing Donglu 6322 2777
Daily 9.30am–10pm Nanjing Road (E)
20, 37

SHAO WAN SHENG

An institution in Shanghai, this shop was originally established as a grocery and snack store during the 1850s by a fisherman from Ningbo. Known as the "Snack King", its signature products are freshwater catches and seafood, such as spiral snails marinated in wine, dried herring and drunken hairy crabs.
J5 414 Nanjing Donglu 6322 4443
Daily 9am–10pm Nanjing Road (E)

CLOTHES

Probably the best place for clothes shopping is Huaihai Zhonglu, the long main road cleaving the French Concession district, where several shops specialize in designer clothes imported from Hong Kong, and independent boutiques can be found down alleyways off the main drag.

Entertainment and Nightlife

BARBAROSSA

This Moroccan-themed bar, next to the pond in Renmin Park, is ideal for unwinding to great music. Happy hour (2pm–8pm) takes some of the sting out of the cocktail prices.

G5 Renmin Park, 231 Nanjing Xilu 6318 0220 Daily 11am–2am People's Square

BIG BAMBOO

bigbamboo.asia

An atypical big, brash sports bar, Big Bamboo is dedicated to beer, Western food, pool and back-to-back sports.

D5 132 Nanyang Lu 6256 2265 Daily 9.30am–2am Jing'an Temple

FENNEL LOUNGE

Besides a small dining area, this venue has a Japanese-style cocktail lounge with music from DJs, as well as live jazz and ethnic music, an inviting picture rounded out by a fine international restaurant.

B6 217 Zhenning Lu 3353 1773 Daily 10am–2am Jiangsu Road

HOUSE OF BLUES & JAZZ

bluesandjazzshanghai.com

This old-timer, just west of the Bund, has long been a stalwart on the Shanghai jazz and blues scene, with a seasoned atmosphere that's strong on wood furnishings. There's a jam session on Sundays; on other nights, the live performances start at 9.30pm.

J6 60 Fuzhou Lu 6323 2779 Tue–Sun 4.30pm–2am Nanjing Road (E)

MAJESTIC THEATRE

This classic theatre was renovated in 2016, enhancing its 1940s looks.

E5 66 Jiangning Lu Nanjing Road (W)

MYST

mystshanghai.com

Three-story club opposite Jing'an Park with a huge dance space, where events include parties with some of the world's top DJs. On the lower floor is a lounge bar, while the top floor is a VIP level.

D6 1123 Yan'an Zhong Lu 6437 9999 Daily 9.30pm til late Jing'an Temple

SHANGHAI CENTRE THEATRE

shanghaicentre.com

One of the highlights of the Shanghai Centre, the theater hosts Chinese and international music, opera, drama and dance, along with regular performances by the Shanghai Acrobatic Theatre.

D5 Shanghai Centre, 1376 Nanjing Xilu 6279 8948 Jing'an Temple

SHANGHAI CONCERT HALL

shanghaiconcerthall.org

Built as the Nanking Theatre in 1930, it was moved, brick by brick, to its present site in 2004. The 1,124-seat concert hall hosts many artists, and a variety of classical music from many countries.

G6 523 Yan'an Donglu 6386 2836 People's Square 46, 71, 123, 454

SHANGHAI GRAND THEATRE

See page 45.

CHINESE OPERA

Chinese opera is entirely unlike Western opera. Foreigners sometimes find it difficult to appreciate at first, but it is worth trying at least once. The singing style is falsetto and the action heavily stylized, but overall it is very colorful and can be highly dramatic, especially if battles are staged using acrobatic techniques. Check the local press for performances.

SKY DOME BAR

radissonblu.com

Crowning the Radisson Blu Hotel Shanghai New World, this 47th-floor bar is one of the top places for truly astral views of Shanghai. There's often live music and snacks are served until 1am.

G5 47th floor, Radisson Blu Hotel Shanghai New World, 88 Nanjing Xilu 6359 9999 Daily 6pm–2am People's Square

STUDIO CITY

If you feel like relaxing at the movies, this six-screen multiplex is a good choice for both Chinese and international films, with some in English. Afternoon showings tend to cost less than evening showings.

E5 10th Floor, Westgate Mall, 1038 Nanjing Xilu 6218 2173 Mon–Thu 9.30am–10pm, Fri–Sun 9.30am–11pm Nanjing Road (W)

Where to Eat

PRICES	
Prices are approximate, based on a 3-course meal for one person.	
$$$	more than 250RMB
$$	100–250RMB
$	under 100RMB

COMMUNE SOCIAL ($$$)

communesocial.com

One of a couple of ventures from Jason Atherton in Shanghai, this wildly popular restaurant serving delicious-looking tapas is a dream, marrying stunning design with a superb menu. Expect to queue as there's no reservations.

E4 511 Jiangning Lu 6047 7638 Tue–Fri noon–2.30, 6–10.30, Sat noon–3 and 6–10.30, Sun noon–3 Changping Road

DIN TAI FUNG ($–$$)

dintaifung.com

No trip to Shanghai is complete without munching on delicious *xiaolongbao* (tender, skinned, steamed dumplings) and Din Tai Fung has an unassailable reputation for turning out some of the best. Watch out for the meat juices inside—they can be scalding.

D5 Shanghai Centre, 1376 Nanjing Xilu 6289 9182 Daily 10am–10pm Jing'an Temple

ELEMENT FRESH ($)

elementfresh.com

Sandwiches, salads and juices are what's on offer at this popular café with several branches in Shanghai. Food is as crisply fresh as the setting, both with a pronounced wholesome bent, attracting a tablet-toting crowd of young white-collar workers and expats.

D5 Room 112, Shanghai Centre, 1376 Nanjing Xilu 6279 8682 Sun–Thu 8am–10pm, Fri & Sat 8am–11pm Jing'an Temple

GONGDELIN ($–$$)

This famous vegetarian restaurant adheres to Buddhist principles, with a variety of vegetable and tofu dishes imitating meat. You may feel it's a bit like eating meat, but the food is entirely meat-free, so your karma will lose none of its sparkle.

F6 445 Nanjing Xilu 6327 0218 Daily lunch, dinner People's Square 20

KATHLEEN'S 5 ($$–$$$)

kathleens5.com

On the fifth floor of the building that was formerly the Shanghai Art Museum (and with a glassed-in rooftop terrace), this smart restaurant serves American-based cuisine that roams the world for elements to mix and match, with local influences. Brunch is served from 11am on weekends.

G6 325 Nanjing Xilu 6327 2221 Mon–Thu 11.30am–midnight, Fri 11.30am–1am, Sat, Sun 11am–1am People's Square 46, 71, 123, 574

LYNN ($–$$)

Excellent, modern and eye-catching Shanghai cuisine in a sharp and stylish environment. Try the crispy duck or the deep-fried spare ribs.

D5 99-1 Xikang Lu 6247 0101 Daily 11.30–2, 5–10.15 Nanjing Road (W)

PINCHUAN ($$–$$$)

pinchuan-china.com

One of Shanghai's best Chuancai restaurants and an established name for the *mala* (spicy and mouth-numbing) cuisine of Sichuan, Pinchuan is a good-looking, smart and surefire choice for the piquant food of West China.

D5 5th fl, Plaza 66, 1266 Nanjing Xilu 6288 8389 10am–10pm West Nanjing Rd

SUMERIAN ($)

sumeriancoffee.com

This small but cheery café does a fine range of coffees for specialist tastes, serious coffeeholics and lovers of the bean as well as snacks for light bites and nibbles.

E5 415 Shanxi Beilu 7.30am–6pm West Nanjing Rd

T8 ($$–$$$)

t8-shanghai.com

At the heart of Xintiandi, this is one of Shanghai's best restaurants for international dishes and pure ambience. Treat yourself to the outstanding dishes and also to the elegant surroundings.

G7 No. 8, North Block, Xintiandi, Lane 181 Taicang Lu 6355 8999 Daily 11.30–2.30, 6.30–11.30 Huangpi Road (S)

VEGETARIAN LIFESTYLE ($–$$)

jujubetree.com

With two other branches in Shanghai, Vegetarian Lifestyle serves up appetizing meat-free, organic and MSG-free dishes that are full of flavor, inventive and stuffed with wholesome goodness.

E5 258 Fengxian Lu 6215 7566 Daily 11.30–9.30 Nanjing Road (W)

WUJIANG LU FOOD STREET ($)

Try not to miss one of Shanghai's food streets when you're in town and Wujiang Lu remains a decent place to find a variety of Chinese, Japanese and Korean eateries, as well as snack food.

E5 Wujiang Lu 10am–10pm West Nanjing Rd

SOUP

In the West it is customary to have soup as a starter or appetizer, but in China soup is generally served toward the end of the meal as a sort of "digestif," and on informal occasions is also a way of helping to finish remains in the rice bowl. At formal functions such as banquets, soup is served in a separate bowl.

The Bund/Waitan

Stretching north from Renmin Lu on the edge of the Old City to the waters of Suzhou Creek, the Bund is Shanghai's premier promenade, a breathtaking vantage point to the glittering towers in Pudong across the Huangpu River.

Top 25

3
4
5
6
7
H
J
Tanggu Lu
Wuchang Lu
Zhapu Lu
SICHUAN BEILU
Beilu
Qipu Lu
Jiangxi
HENAN BEILU
Shanxi Beilu
Tiantong Lu
Fujian Beilu
Shanxi Beilu
Tiantong Road
Tiantong Lu
Shanghai Post Museum
Suzhou Beilu
Suzhou Creek
Suzhou Beilu
Suzhou Nanlu
Suzhou
Nanlu
Hong Kong Lu
Yuanmingyuan Lu
WAIBAIDU BRIDGE
BEIJING DONGLU
Zhonglu
ZHONGLU
Huqiu
Yuan-mingyuan Lu
Monument to the People's Heroes
Rockbund Art Museum
Huangpu Park
Jiangxi
SICHUAN
Bank of China
Dianchi Lu
NANJING DONGLU
Fairmont Peace Hotel
ZHONGSHAN DONG 1-LU
Chen Yi Monument
Jiujiang Lu
BUND SIGHTSEEING TUNNEL
ZHONGLU
Hankou Lu
Zhonglu
Zhonglu
The Bund
HENAN
Fuzhou Lu
Shandong
Zhongshan
Fujian Zhonglu
Guangdong Lu
Wuhu Lu
Guangdong Lu
Jiangxi
Sichuan Zhonglu
YAN'AN DONGLU TUNNEL
Shanghai Gallery of Art
YAN'AN DONGLU
Ninghai Donglu
Fujian Nanlu
0
400 m
0
400 yds

The Bund/Waitan

Around Suzhou Creek

TOP 25

HIGHLIGHTS

- Waibaidu Bridge
- Former British Consulate
- Russian Consulate
- Astor House Hotel
- Broadway Mansions
- Shanghai Post Museum

TIP

- The highlight of this neighborhood is to wander around Suzhou Creek, bumping into concession-era architecture, art deco apartment blocks, churches, post offices and other distinguished buildings from Shanghai's past.

Suzhou Creek used to represent much that was unattractive in Shanghai's rush to develop. Today, it's a sign of how the city is cleaning up its act.

The Colonial Period Suzhou Creek separated the British and American Concession, and the banks close to the Huangpu River have some architectural survivors from this time. The Broadway Mansions Hotel, at 20 Suzhou Beilu, is in an art deco masterpiece (1934; ▷ 110). Also on the north bank, the former Astor House Hotel, at 15 Huangpu Lu, is a historic survivor, as is the Russian Consulate opposite, which is one of Shanghai's most notable buildings, with its red roof and waterside perch. The twin-span steel Waibaidu (Garden) Bridge, which crosses over the creek alongside Huangpu Park (▷ 63),

Clockwise from left: Distinctive architecture along the banks of the creek; Suzhou Creek artists' quarter; a new apartment block on the creekside; vessels line the sides of the creek and traffic passes along the middle; the Russian Consulate building

dates from 1907, replacing a wooden bridge. The old Shanghai Post Office building, at 250 Suzhou Beilu, houses the intriguing Shanghai Post Museum.

Troubled Waters From its source in Tai Hu (Lake Tai) close to Suzhou, the creek flows east through some of China's most polluted territory before debouching into the Huangpu River at the north end of the Bund. By 1998, when the first clean-up measures were introduced, Suzhou Creek's water had become a black open sewer. Those who lived beside the creek—a fate reserved for the poor—could not open their windows in summer, so bad was the smell. The Suzhou Creek Rehabilitation Project has changed things for the better. More needs to be done, but fish are returning.

THE BASICS

- H5–K5
- Suzhou Nanlu and Suzhou Beilu
- Nanjing Road (E)
- 20, 55, 65

The Bund

TOP 25

HIGHLIGHTS

- Panoramic views
- Waterfront European-style buildings
- Boat trips on the Huangpu River (▷ 60)

TIP

- The Bund shows different faces of itself during the day: Early morning tai chi practitioners give way to rush-hour crowds, then a period of calm before the lunchtime and afternoon strollers emerge. Evening, the time for leisure crowds, is followed by those out to view the lights.

Arriving by ship from Europe or America in the 1930s, the expatriate's first view of Shanghai would have been the waterfront street known as the Bund, a grand slice of the colonial world.

Waitan The Bund (meaning "waterfront" or "embankment") is now known as Waitan or Zhongshan Dong Yilu (or 1-Lu). It runs along the Huangpu River from Suzhou Creek in the north to Yan'an Lu in the south. The buildings lining it date from the early 20th century and are largely Western in style. The Bund is where modern Shanghai began and it remains the city's grandest display. A "must do" activity is to stroll the Bund after dark, when the illuminated waterfront and the view to Pudong create a memorable vista.

Clockwise from left: A flag flying atop the Customs House clock tower; statue of Chen Yi, the first mayor of Shanghai; the Bund viewed from the Riverside Promenade; tai chi exercises; a bronze lion outside the Hong Kong and Shanghai Bank

The Buildings Although changes have been made—the trams have gone, as have the old "go-downs," or warehouses, and statues of foreigners—the Bund would be recognizable to a 1930s resident. A walk from south to north would begin with the Shanghai Club at No. 3, which claimed to have the longest bar in the world. The domed building at No. 12 was the Hong Kong and Shanghai Bank, built in 1923; it is worth popping in to look at the ceiling mosaics. Next door, surmounted by a clock once known as Big Ching, is the Customs House of 1927. Next to the main building of the Fairmont Peace Hotel (▷ 62) on the corner of Nanjing Lu (Nanking Road) is the Bank of China (1937). No. 27 was the headquarters of Jardine Matheson, and No. 33 was the old British Consulate.

THE BASICS

- J6–K5
- Zhongshan Dong 1-Lu
- Various restaurants and cafés
- Nanjing Road (E)
- Few

Huangpu Riverboat Tour

TOP 25

HIGHLIGHTS

- Fabulous panoramas of both the Bund and Lujiazui in Pudong
- Confluence with the mighty Yangtze River
- Yangpu Bridge

TIP

- If you don't have the time or the money, try one of the cross-river ferries instead, a fun, waterborne way of getting to Pudong and which you can think of as an inexpensive micro-cruise on the river.

The Huangpu and Yangtze rivers are the original reasons for Shanghai's prosperity. A river cruise along the Huangpu will show aspects of this huge city you might not otherwise see.

Two Rivers The Yangtze is the longest river in China. Rising in the Tibetan Plateau, it meanders across the country, most famously passing the Three Gorges. The Huangpu, only 68 miles (110km) in length, runs from Dianshan Lake and empties into the Yangtze River 17 miles (28km) downstream. Its average width through the city is 1,300ft (400m) and its average depth 26ft (8m). Large ships were able to enter the wide mouth of the Yangtze, make the short journey up the Huangpu and unload at the wharves along the Bund. The goods were

Paddle steamer on the Huangpu River

transported by barges along Suzhou Creek and then on canals for distribution through China.

Touring the Huangpu Boat tours leave from Shiliupu Wharf in Old Town, south of the intersection between Remin Lu and Zhongshan Dong 1-Lu. The shortest trips merely journey past the International Cruise Passenger Terminal and back, while the longest trip is the three-and-a-half-hour return journey to Wusongkou at the mouth of the Yangtze River. If you travel first class, the trip to Wusongkou and back is comfortable. You first pass Suzhou Creek, then the new Shanghai Port International Ferry Terminal and Yangpu Bridge. You will also pass Fuxing Island, where Chiang Kai Shek made his last stand before fleeing to Taiwan. Finally, you meet the Yangtze, before returning.

THE BASICS

K7/L5

Shiliupu Wharf in Old Town, close to Yuyuan on Zhongshan Dong 1-Lu (K7)

6374 4461

Cruises depart daily every 2 hours or so 11am–9.30pm

Bar on board ship

55, 65

Good

Expensive—tickets from the tourist information center on the Bund near the pier

Performances often given on river cruise

Fairmont Peace Hotel

The hotel's Dragon Phoenix Restaurant (left); the hotel's Old Jazz Band (right)

THE BASICS

fairmont.com/peace-hotel-shanghai

J5

20 Nanjing Donglu

6321 6888

All year

Café, bars and restaurants on premises

Nanjing Road (E)

37, 42, 55, 65

Good

Free, unless you spend the night

HIGHLIGHTS

- Art deco architecture
- Art deco details in the lobby

The Fairmont Peace Hotel is the most iconic art deco building in Shanghai. During its heyday, this was the place to stay and the patina of its pyramid roof is a distinctive Bund image.

The Sassoons Of the many families of Sephardic Jews, the most famous is the Sassoon family. Fleeing an intolerant Baghdad in the 18th century to make a fortune in Bombay, they then proceeded to buy warehouses in Shanghai. Successive generations invested in the port, but it was Victor Sassoon who built the well-known landmark on the Bund now known as the Fairmont Peace Hotel. Though it represents the hated era of foreign domination, many new skyscrapers copy its distinctive pyramidical roof design.

The Cathay Victor Sassoon had visions of a skyscraper as a business headquarters and wanted to include a hotel. Today's Fairmont Peace Hotel, originally the Cathay, dates from 1930, with art deco ironwork and high ceilings inside and looking like a smaller Empire State Building outside. The lowest four floors were reserved for offices; the remainder were given over to what Victor hoped would be the finest hotel in the East. It had the best technology and service that the period could offer, while the Horse & Hounds Bar became the most fashionable rendezvous in the city. Renovated and reopened as the Fairmont Peace Hotel, it once again attracts the in-crowd.

More to See

HUANGPU PARK

At the northern end of the Bund near the bridge, this is the infamous park where a notice was said to forbid entry to "Dogs and Chinese" (the wording was not exactly like that, in fact). It is a pleasant park with an ugly monument, beneath which is a small museum about the features of old Shanghai.

K5 Zhongshan Dong 1-Lu (the Bund) Summer daily 6am–10pm; winter 6–6 Nanjing Road (E) None Free

ROCKBUND ART MUSEUM (RAM)

rockbundartmuseum.org

An acclaimed contemporary gallery in the former Royal Asiatic Society building, it displays photography and art. The museum has no permanent collection, with temporary exhibitions on display. One of the highlights is the delightful art deco lines of the building. The stairwell is lovely, as are the windows, while the whole edifice is a study in art deco elegance.

J5 120 Huqiu Lu 3310 9985 Tue–Sat 10–6 Moderate Nanjing Road (E)

SHANGHAI GALLERY OF ART

threeonthebund.com

This exclusive gallery, in the prestigious Three on the Bund shopping, dining and entertainment complex, displays contemporary art.

J6 3rd floor, Three on the Bund, Zhongshan Dong 1-Lu 6321 5757 See website for exhibition dates Free Nanjing Road (E)

YUANMINGYUAN LU

The elegant, grand and restored Yuanmingyuan Lu west of the Bund is a major piece of Shanghai heritage, with some outstanding examples of art deco and historic architecture. Look out for the YWCA building, the astonishing brickwork of the Chinese Baptist Publication building and the grand former British Consulate building.

J5 Yuanmingyuan Lu 24hr Nanjing Rd (E)

Early morning exercises in Huangpu Park

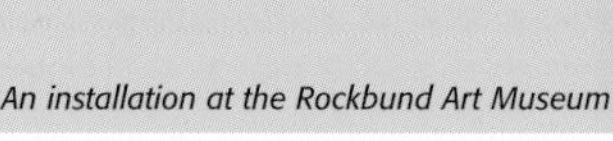

An installation at the Rockbund Art Museum

The Bund

The very symbol of 19th-century foreign interventions in China, the Bund (▷ 58–59) was where the story of modern Shanghai began.

DISTANCE: 1.2 miles (2km) **ALLOW:** Up to 1 hour

START

SUZHOU CREEK (▷ 56)
K5 Nanjing Road (E)

❶ From Waibaidu Bridge at Suzhou Creek, walk south down the west side of Zhongshan Dong 1-Lu. One of the first buildings you will see is the former British Consulate, behind the gates at No. 33.

❷ The House of Roosevelt, at 1920s Beaux-Arts icon No. 27, boasts a climate-controlled wine cellar.

❸ The Peace Hotel (▷ 62) stands on the corner of Nanjing Donglu. Over the road is a second wing of the Peace Hotel, once the Palace Hotel and now the Swatch Art Peace Hotel.

❹ Continue south, crossing Jiujiang Lu, Hankou Lu and Fuzhou Lu, taking in details on buildings like the Customs House at No. 13 and the former Hong Kong and Shanghai Bank at No. 12.

❺ On the south side of Guangdong Lu, at No. 3, is the stellar Three on the Bund shopping, dining and cultural complex.

❻ Cross over Zhongshan Dong 1-Lu, and go north along the Bund's waterfront promenade, affording you a different view of the buildings you have just passed, and views to Pudong's skyscrapers.

❼ At the north end of the Bund, stroll through Huangpu Park (▷ 63), then cross Waibaidu Bridge to look out over to the historic red-roofed Russian Consulate building to the east.

END

WAIBAIDU BRIDGE (▷ 56)
K5 Nanjing Road (E)

Shopping

BLUE SHANGHAI WHITE

blueshanghaiwhite.com

This teeny boutique is a breath of fresh air off the Bund, with its eye-catching collection of elegantly painted Chinese ceramics which are perfect as gifts or for decorating your home.

J6 Room 103, 17 Fuzhou Lu 6323 0856 Daily 10.30–6.30 Nanjing Road (E)

SILK KING

One of Shanghai's most popular silk outlets for silk by the meter or tailor-made clothes. Silk King also has in-house tailors who can set you up with a figure-hugging *cheongsam* or a smart Chinese-style jacket.

J5 588 Nanjing Donglu 6321 2193 Nanjing Road (E)

SUZHOU COBBLERS

suzhou-cobblers.com

Choose from a wide range of exquisite hand-embroidered Chinese silk slippers, or pick one of the handbags that come in a variety of colors and designs, for a reminder of your time in Shanghai.

J6 Room 101, 17 Fuzhou Lu 6321 7087 Daily 10–6.30 Nanjing Road (E)

Entertainment and Nightlife

BAR ROUGE

bar-rouge-shanghai.com

One of the coolest cocktail bars in town, Bar Rouge attracts a vibrant, fun-loving crowd that is here for the phenomenal views across the water to Lujiazui and a party atmosphere ramped up by DJs after midnight.

J6 18 Zhongshan Dong 1-Lu (the Bund) 6339 1199 Mon–Thu 3pm–2am, Fri, Sat 3pm–4am; special brunch Sat–Sun noon–4pm Nanjing Road (E) 37, 42, 55, 65

GLAM BAR

m-restaurantgroup.com/glam

Situated on the 7th floor of the 1930s Nissin Shipping Building, Glam is a gorgeous place for an evening cocktail or fine international cuisine above the Bund, with fantastic views and a cool, artsy vibe.

J6 7th fl, 20 Guangdong Lu 6350 9988 Daily 5pm–late Nanjing Rd (E) 37, 42, 55, 65

SIR ELLY'S TERRACE

shanghai.peninsula.com

Offering panoramic views across the Huangpu River, Suzhou Creek and Pudong, this U-shaped rooftop bar on top of the Peninsula Shanghai (▷ 112) has the Bund's largest terrace. Cocktails and light snacks are served in style. It throngs with Shanghai's elite in the summer but, as it's al fresco, the terrace is closed during the winter months and opens again in spring. Dress is smart casual whatever the weather.

J5 14th floor, 32 Zhongshan Dong 1-Lu (the Bund) 2327 6756 Sun–Thu 5pm–midnight, Fri–Sat 5pm–1am Nanjing Road (E)

Where to Eat

PRICES

Prices are approximate, based on a 3-course meal for one person.

$$$ more than 250RMB
$$ 100–250RMB
$ under 100RMB

AJISEN ($)

ajisen.com.cn

Ajisen's Japanese noodles long ago developed a loyal following across the entire land. Service is efficient, although you may have to wait for a table. The photo menu makes choosing your food easy if your language skills are limited; you pay at the start of the meal.

J5 479 Nanjing Donglu 6360 7194 Daily 10–10 Nanjing Road (E)

GRAND BRASSERIE ($$$)

waldorfastoriashanghai.com

One of three restaurants at the extremely sophisticated and opulent Waldorf Astoria hotel, the Grand Brasserie offers chic but casual all-day dining with an East-meets-West menu. Its champagne brunch on Sundays is worth getting up for.

J6 2 Zhongshan Dong 1-Lu (the Bund) 6322 9988 Daily 6–10.30, 11.30–3, 5.30–11 Nanjing Road (E) 37, 42, 55, 65

JEAN GEORGES ($$–$$$)

jean-georges.com

Offering an excellent selection of French-Asian fusion fare in a very stylish setting, this is one of Shanghai's best restaurants for Western cuisine It's one of several Jean Georges worldwide.

J6 4th floor, Three on the Bund, 3 Zhongshan Dong 1-Lu 6321 7733 Daily 11.30–2.30, 6–11 (Sat–Sun 11.30–3) Nanjing Road (E)

M ON THE BUND ($$)

m-restaurantgroup.com

With its lovely outdoor terrace, the long-standing M on the Bund remains one of Shanghai's best dining experiences, serving European dishes with fine views as standard, but you'll need to reserve ahead to secure a decent table outside.

J6 7th floor, 20 Guangdong Lu 6350 9988 Mon–Fri 11.30–2.30, 6–10.30, Sat–Sun 11.30–3, 3–5 Nanjing Road (E)

MR & MRS BUND ($–$$)

mmbund.com

French food with a fusion twist and views across to Pudong from this uber-cool restaurant on the 6th floor of the Bund 18 building. Arrive early or make a reservation to get a window table.

J6 6th floor, 18 Zhongshan Dong 1-Lu (the Bund) 6323 9898 Daily 5.30–10.30pm (Thu–Sat to 1.30am) Nanjing Road (E) 37, 42, 55, 65

SHANGHAI GRANDMOTHER ($)

If you want no-nonsense, deservedly popular Chinese dishes, this place rarely disappoints in a neighborhood flooded with self-conscious restaurants. There's little fancy on the menu, only tasty, down-to-earth Chinese favorites.

J6 70 Fuzhou Lu 6321 6613 Daily 10.30–9.30 Nanjing Road (E)

DUMPLINGS

Like north China's famous dumplings, Shanghai's signature dish—copied across the nation—is *xiaolongbao* (pronounced "seeyaolongbough"). Small, steamed, plump dumplings, *xiaolongbao* come in a variety of fillings, from pork to crab meat, arriving at the table in steamers. Bite carefully, as the meat juice can be scalding.

Old Town/Nanshi

The rickety Old Town contains the Yu Garden, the Yuyuan Bazaar, Huxinting Tea House, as well as several notable temples and antiques markets—an atmospheric escape from Shanghai's more frantic districts.

Top 25

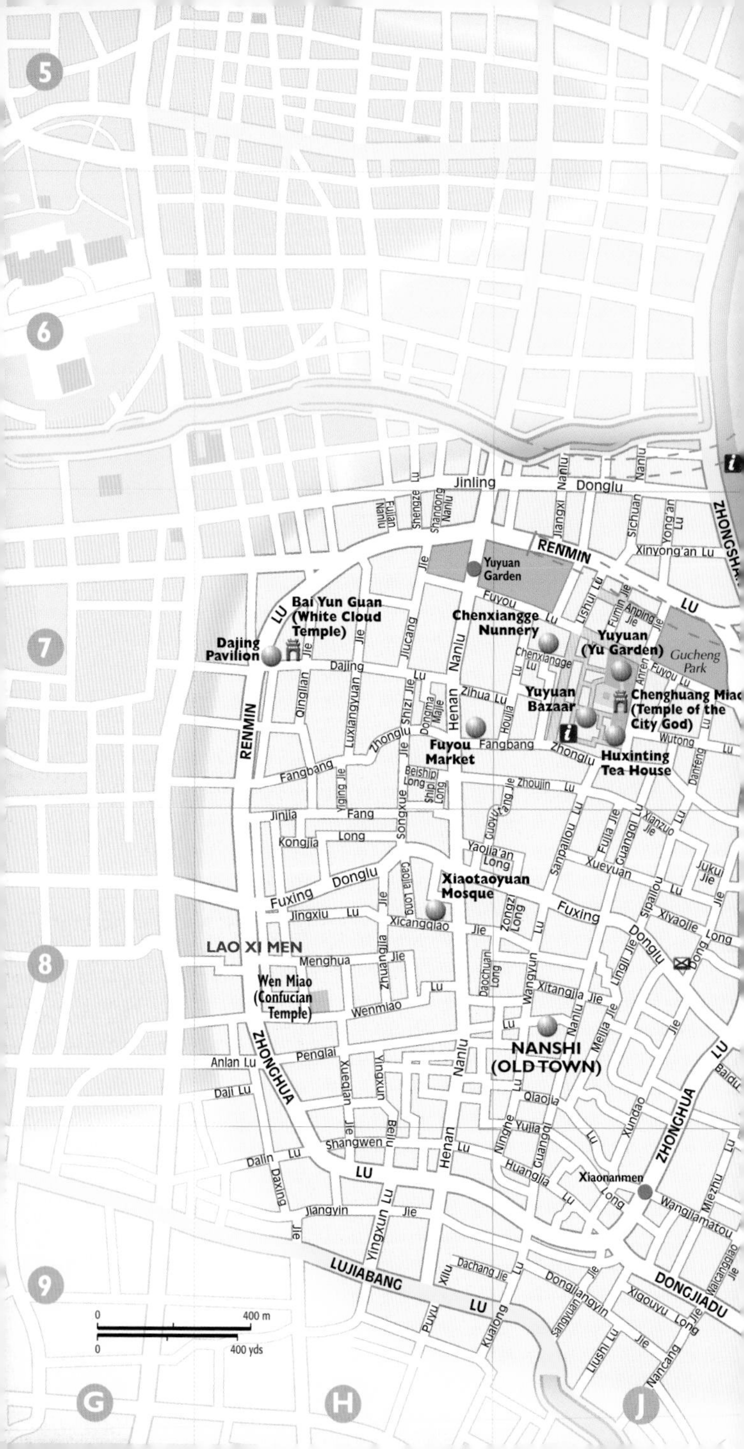

5
6
7
8
9
G
H
J
Jinling
Donglu
RENMIN
LU
Yuyuan Garden
Bai Yun Guan (White Cloud Temple)
Dajing Pavilion
Chenxiangge Nunnery
Yuyuan (Yu Garden)
Gucheng Park
Yuyuan Bazaar
Chenghuang Miao (Temple of the City God)
Huxinting Tea House
Fuyou Market
Xiaotaoyuan Mosque
LAO XI MEN
Wen Miao (Confucian Temple)
NANSHI (OLD TOWN)
ZHONGHUA
Xiaonanmen
LUJIABANG
DONGJIADU
Fuxing
Dajing
Fangbang
Zhonglu
0
400 m
400 yds

Old Town/Nanshi

Huxinting Tea House

TOP 25

HIGHLIGHTS

- Charming building in entertaining location
- Cooling on hot days

TIP

- When the waiter or waitress refills your tea cup, tapping the index and second fingers of your right hand is a traditional way to indicate "thank you" for being served tea—the gesture represents the kowtow that everyone had to do in the presence of the emperor.

The delightful old teahouse, in its watery setting in the middle of a lake, is the focal point of the Old Town. It fits in with the China of popular imagination, a China that has all but disappeared.

Tea Drinking Tea is widely produced throughout central and southern China and is also widely consumed in everyday life–taxi drivers often keep a jar with them, half filled with leaves to which boiling water is added throughout the day; there will probably be tea in your hotel room; and when people meet, or at an official function, tea will certainly be served at some point. In the past, every town had several teahouses, where conversation was an adjunct to an appreciation of good teas. However, an appreciation of fine teas and the art of tea

Clockwise from left: People negotiating the Nine Zig-Zag Bridge to the teahouse; relaxing with tea and snacks; the teahouse illuminated at night

drinking in its ceremonial form, where such matters as the quality of the water used are much considered, has largely vanished.

Huxinting The Huxinting Tea House, which is surrounded by a small lake, is truly the hub of the Old Town. Its precise origins are not entirely clear, but it dates from some time during the Ming dynasty, was renovated as a brokerage house in 1784, and became a teahouse in 1856. It was originally part of both the Temple of the City God (▷ 75) and Yuyuan (▷ 74). As Shanghai prospered, parts of the garden, including the teahouse, were purchased by local merchants, who used it as a meeting place for conducting business. A building of great charm, it is approached via the Nine Zig-Zag Bridge, over waters glittering with goldfish.

THE BASICS

yuyuantm.com.cn
J7
257 Yuyuan Lu
6373 6950
Daily 8am–9pm
Plenty of restaurants nearby, in the Old Town
Yuyuan Garden
14, 26
None
Moderate
Tea ceremony performed in the evening

Old Town

TOP 25

HIGHLIGHTS

- A hint of the atmosphere of old China
- Excellent snack food and shops

TIP

- Most visitors to the Old Town focus on its northern section, around Yuyuan and the Huxinting Tea House. But there's much more to the district than this, and, if anything, the other parts are more authentic.

It's an unexpected pleasure to discover, amid the high-rise modernity, an old Chinese town—the original Shanghai. In its narrow streets you can absorb something of the atmosphere and bustle of traditional China.

History Until the Treaty of Nanking in 1842, Shanghai was a moderately important walled town concentrated in the area now called Nanshi. The walls were pulled down in 1912 to provide better access for shops and traders, but even now the area is self-contained and the route of the old walls can be traced along Renmin Lu and Zhonghua Lu. A single chunk of wall survives at the Dajing Pavilion on Dajing Lu. Some of Shanghai's ancient temples survive in the Old Town, including the Wen Miao

Clockwise from left: The busy Yuyuan Bazaar; modern lighting illuminates the renovated stores at night; an example of a traditional building in the Old Town; passing a flower stall at the Bird and Flower Market

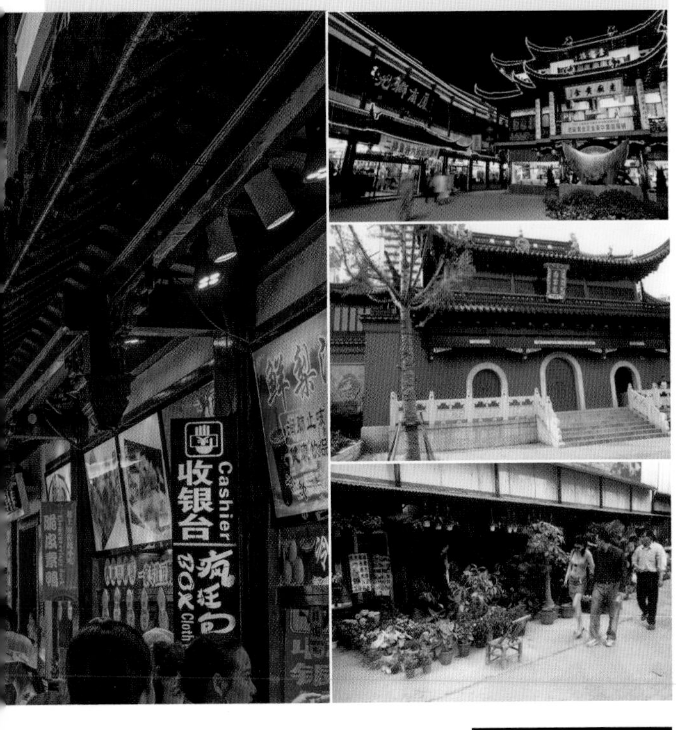

(Confucius Temple; ▷ 76), the Chenghuang Miao (▷ 75) and the Chenxiangge Nunnery (▷ 75). The signature sight is the Yuyuan (▷ 74) and the surrounding bazaar.

Today The Old Town has been spared the over-development that has robbed Shanghai of so much history. Although some rebuilding has taken place, the old Chinese town retains its prewar atmosphere, stuffed with narrow lanes hung above with drying washing. The disheveled streets are filled with specialist shops selling walking sticks or tea, and markets overflowing with food, collectibles and knick-knacks. There are several antiques markets, but you'll need a discerning eye to select genuine items. The Yuyuan Bazaar (▷ 76) brims with shops selling traditional gift items.

THE BASICS

H7–J9

Plenty of restaurants in the area

Yuyuan Garden

None

Free

Yuyuan

TOP 25

A willow overhangs a pond in the garden (left); detail of a building (right)

THE BASICS

yugarden.com.cn
J7
218 Anren Jie, Old Town
Daily summer 8.30–5.30; winter 8.30–5 (last entry 30 minutes before closing time)
Plenty of restaurants nearby, in the Old Town
Yuyuan Garden
26
Moderate

HIGHLIGHTS

- Rockeries, bridges and pavilions
- Miniature fish-filled lake and pavilion

TIP

- Yuyuan can be crowded, particularly on summer weekends. Try to visit early in the morning or at lunchtime.

Shanghai has its surprises. Hidden away in a well-tended corner of the Old Town is one of the finest surviving classical Chinese gardens in the land.

The Pan Family The Yuyuan, or Yu Garden, has a long history. It was created in the mid-16th century by Pan Yunduan as an act of filial affection for his father. Pan, a native of Shanghai who had been in public service in Sichuan province, must have been a wealthy and influential figure, for the garden takes up almost 12 acres (5ha), a large chunk of the Old Town. By the time it was completed in 1587, however, Pan's father had died, and although additions were made to the garden from time to time, it suffered from neglect. Twice in the 19th century it was used as headquarters—in 1842 by the British Land Force and in the 1850s by the Small Swords Society, dedicated to the restoration of the Ming dynasty.

Today's Garden The Yu Garden exemplifies the classic Ming garden, where rock gardens, bridges and ponds surround pavilions and corridors to create an illusion of a natural landscape. In reality, although the materials are the work of nature, the design is obviously the work of people. But what is important is the "harmony of scale," its beauty lying in the intricate design, which would have permitted tranquil contemplation in a comparatively small area. An unusual feature is the sculpted dragon that curls around the top of the garden wall.

More to See

BAI YUN GUAN (WHITE CLOUD TEMPLE)

Relocated several years ago from its former location to the west of the Old Town, this Taoist temple is modern in feel, but makes an interesting contrast to the local Buddhist temples.

H7 239 Dajing Lu Daily 8–4.30 Dashijie Inexpensive

CHENGHUANG MIAO (TEMPLE OF THE CITY GOD)

The Temple of the City God has been reconstructed more than 20 times since it was founded in 1403, but its popularity with devotees, especially those praying for wealth and prosperity, remains undiminished. The hall of the City God is to the rear of the building, beyond the inner courtyard, where you may see red-robed trainee monks, a reminder that this is very much a working temple.

J7 249 Fangbang Zhonglu (at Yu Garden) Daily 8.30–4.30 Yuyuan Garden None Inexpensive

CHENXIANGGE NUNNERY

This small Buddhist temple belonged to the Pan family, who built Yuyuan. It takes its name from an eaglewood statue of Guanyin, which gives off a resinous scent in damp weather.

J7 2a Chenxiangge Lu Daily 7–5 Yuyuan Garden 11, 24, 26 None Inexpensive

COOL DOCKS

thecooldocks.com

This warehouse-and-shikumen area near the river was designed as a rival to Xintiandi; it never quite took off, but is worth exploring for its shops and excellent restaurants.

K9 479 Zhongshan Nanlu Xiaonanmen

DONGJIADU CATHEDRAL

Built by Spanish Jesuits in 1853 as the St. Xavier cathedral, in a style reminiscent of Iberian colonial baroque, Dongjiadu is the oldest Catholic church in Shanghai and stands outside the southeastern

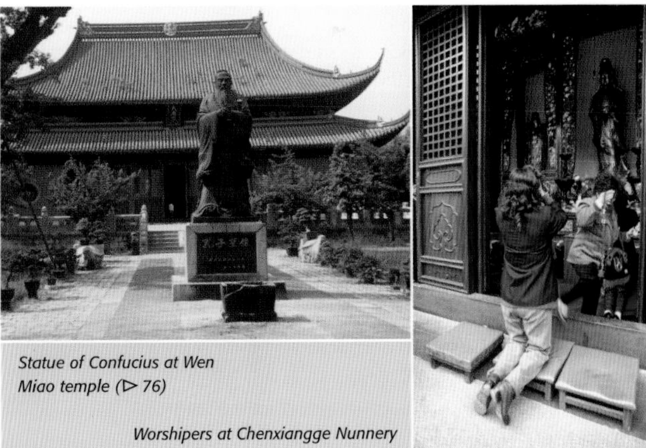

Statue of Confucius at Wen Miao temple (▷ 76)

Worshipers at Chenxiangge Nunnery

edge of the Old Town. It is a working church, with Mass in Chinese said daily.
K9 185 Dongjiadu Lu Nanpu Bridge Free

FUYOU MARKET
One of Shanghai's most well-known antiques markets, this place is at its busiest early on Sundays, but there's a permanent collection of stalls here that are open daily. Prices can be quite high, so haggling is a must.
H7 459 Fangbang Zhonglu Daily 9–5 Restaurants Yuyuan Garden 11, 14, 26, 66, 306 None Free

WEN MIAO
confuciantemple.com
Typical of Confucius temples with its main hall, the Dacheng Hall, dedicated to the sage, the few worshipers points to the decline of Confucianism, relative to Buddhism or Christianity; although the influence of Confucius in China remains immense. A used-book market gets up and going here on Sunday mornings.
H8 215 Wenmiao Lu Daily 8.30–4.30 Laoximen 11, 14, 26 None Inexpensive

XIAOTAOYUAN MOSQUE
chinaislam.net.cn
Worth a visit to appreciate the multi-religious character of Shanghai, this small mosque was built in 1917.
H8 52 Xiaotaoyuan Lu Daily, any time until 8.30pm Laoximen

YUYUAN BAZAAR
yuyuantm.com.cn
Despite its ceremonial gateways, rosewood lanterns and pagodas with sloping eaves, it was built in the 1990s. It's one of the best places to shop for souvenirs, though not for genuine antiques. (Haggling is expected, but you may get a better price in the smaller shops on Fangbang Zhonglu.)
J7 Streets around Yuyuan Daily 7–6 Yuyuan Garden 26 None

Chopsticks for sale at the Yuyuan Bazaar

The entrance to Yuyuan Bazaar

Old Town

Many old buildings survive in the Nanshi district, Shanghai's once-walled Old Town, and you will see some of them on this walk.

DISTANCE: 1.5 miles (2.4km) **ALLOW:** 1 hour (not including stops)

START

DONGMEN LU
K8 55, 65

❶ Start at Dongmen Lu, the site of the old east gate to the Chinese town, close to the Huangpu River. Walk westward and pass Waixiangua Jie (Salty Melon Street), with its local street market.

❷ Continue to Zhonghua Lu and cross the street to enter Fangbang Zhonglu.

❸ Continue past a variety of shops until an old Chinese arch appears to the right. This is the entrance to the Temple of the City God (▷ 75).

❹ Go through the arch and make your way among the shops and restaurants until you come to the lake and the Huxinting Tea House (▷ 70–71), near the entrance to the Yuyuan (Yu Garden; ▷ 74).

❺ Bear right around the lake and then turn left to wander among the narrow streets before bearing right to leave this area and emerge into Fuyou Lu.

❻ Turn left here and left again into Jiujiaochang Lu. A street on the right (Chenxiangge Lu) takes you to a small neighborhood temple, the Chenxiangge Nunnery (▷ 75).

❼ Return to Jiujiaochang Lu, walk south to Fangbang Zhonglu and then turn right to browse through the shops of Shanghai Old Street (▷ 78) and take a peek at the Fuyou Market (▷ 76), busiest on Sundays.

FUYOU MARKET
H7 Yuyuan Garden

END

Shopping

HUABAO BUILDING ANTIQUES MARKET

Housed in the basement of a building close to the Yu Garden, this is one of the city's best sources of quality antiques and knickknacks, so make sure you leave plenty of time to explore this little treasure trove.

J7 265 Fangbang Zhonglu Daily 9–5.30 Yuyuan Garden 42, 64

SHANGHAI OLD STREET

Not nearly as old as its name implies, having been redeveloped as recently as 1999, the eastern segment of Fangbang Zhonglu at least creates a fairly convincing illusion of being old, thanks to its small shops selling antiques, crafts, bric-a-brac and tea. It remains an excellent place to find souvenirs and gifts and, with the closure of nearby Dongtai Lu Antique Market, there are better pickings than before, but ensure you always weigh up any potential purchases with a shrewd eye and, of course, assume that everything is reproduction.

J7 Fangbang Zhonglu Yuyuan Garden 26

SHILIUPU FABRIC MARKET

The former Dongjiadu fabric market has moved to many locations since closing several years ago and most recently came to these indoor premises in the Old Town. There's a large selection of raw textiles to choose from (wool, silk, linen, cotton and others), sold from scores of stalls. You can also have clothes, including suits, made to measure here, although you may have to hunt around to find someone who speaks English.

J8 2 Zhonghua Lu Daily 8.30–6 Yuyuan Garden

SILK WORLD

This emporium on the edge of the Yuyuan Bazaar sells all manner of silk products, from shirts and jackets to quilts and embroidered pajamas.

J7 125 Jiujiaochang Lu 2302 9374 Daily 9–5.50 Yuyuan Garden 26

SOUTH BUND FABRIC MARKET

A wonderful labyrinth of stalls laden with every type of material, from wool, cotton and linen to silk and cashmere, this famous market is the place to go if you are after an inexpensive suit or dress. Tailors are on hand to measure you there and then, while seamstresses will run up the garment in 24 hours if you need it that quickly.

J9 399 Lujiabang Lu 6377 2236 Daily 9–6 Nanpu Bridge

BUYING ANTIQUES

It is illegal to export anything older than 150 years. A red seal on an antique will tell you that it is genuine and exportable.
If there is no red seal, there's no sure-fire method of knowing what you are buying other than to really inspect the object in question. Some imitations are of a high standard but are often marked on the bottom as being authentic reproductions. This is information the salesperson is unlikely to volunteer but, if you like the item, it will still be cheaper than the real thing. A simple rule of thumb when buying antiques in Shanghai is simply to purchase the object that takes your fancy, because you like it and aim to hang on to it, with the assumption that it is a reproduction piece. It is not a good idea to purchase anything with the ambition of selling it on, unless you know precisely what you are looking for and are confident in discerning an original from a fake.

Where to Eat

PRICES

Prices are approximate, based on a 3-course meal for one person.
$$$ more than 250RMB
$$ 100–250RMB
$ under 100RMB

HUXINTING TEA HOUSE ($)

yuyuantm.com.cn

There's nowhere in Shanghai quite like this venerable teahouse (▷ 70) for experiencing a taste of Old China, even if popularity has brought in the crowds.

J7 257 Yuyuan Lu 6373 6950 Daily 8am–9pm 14, 26

LAO FANDIAN (SHANGHAI OLD RESTAURANT $$–$$$)

yuyuantm.com.cn

Something of an institution, this modernized version of an old restaurant (the name means "old restaurant") serves Shanghai dishes (including noodles, and seafood according to the season) and is conveniently situated in the Old Town.

J7 242 Fuyou Lu 6311 1777 Daily lunch, dinner Yuyuan Garden 26

LU BO LANG ($$)

International movers and shakers, celebrities and ordinary folk alike pile into this signature Old Town traditional eatery on the edge of the Yuyuan lake. Celebrity status has made the Shanghainese food a little touristy and the bills higher, but the experience is worthwhile.

J7 115 Yuyuan Lu 6328 0602 Daily 7.30am–8.15pm Yuyuan Garden 26

NAN XIANG ($–$$)

The best place in the city to try *xiaolongbao* (Shanghai-style steamed dumplings). These are stuffed with various fillings: vegetables, crab, pork. All three floors here are usually busy, so be ready to wait for a table.

J7 85 Yuyuan Lu 6355 4206 Daily lunch, dinner Yuyuan Garden 26

OLD SHANGHAI TEA HOUSE ($)

Escape the busyness of the Yuyuan Bazaar to this small island of peace and sanity. The teahouse is awash with 1920s memorabilia, with everything from cookie tins to old telephones. The staff wear Mandarin gowns or silk *qipaos* and serve the teas on lacquered trays. Snacks of sour plums, muskmelon seeds and quail eggs can be enjoyed alongside the tea.

J7 385 Fangbang Zhonglu 5382 1202 Daily 9–9 42, 66, 969

SONGYUELOU ($)

Dating back to 1910, this is one of Shanghai's best-known vegetarian restaurants, cooking up a range of mock-meat dishes (the traditional way vegetarian food is prepared here). Dishes are inexpensive, and tasty.

J7 99 Jiujiaochang Lu 6355 3630 Daily 11am–7.30pm Yuyuan Garden 26

LOCAL SNACKS

One of the specialties of the region is *Ningbo* or "pigeon egg" dumplings, little balls of sticky rice enclosing a delicious sweet *osmanthus* paste. Another snack is *zhong zhi*, sticky rice with meat wrapped in a lotus leaf. To find these and other delicious snacks, stop in the Old Town—both in the area of the Huxinting Tea House and on the streets around it, where there are many small restaurants and stalls.

茶
TEA

Hongkou

A rambling district north of Suzhou Creek, Hongkou incorporates the former International Concession. It later became a popular haunt of many liberal and revolutionary writers, artists and intellectuals.

Top 25

Tomb of Lu Xun
Hongkou Stadium
Hongkou Football Stadium
Memorial Hall of Lu Xun
Former Residence of Lu Xun
HONGKOU
Duolun Lu Cultural Street
Dongbaoxing Road
Children's Park
Hailun Road
North Sichuan Road
Jiefang Theatre
BAOSHAN LU
SICHUAN BEILU
HAINING LU
WUSONG LU
SIPING
Wujing Lu
Qiujiang Zhilu
Dongxinmin Lu
1
2
3
4
5
H
J
K

Lu Xun Park
Quyang Road
DALIAN XILU
Tianbao Xilu
Quyang Lu
Qingyang Lu
Xiangde Lu
SIPING LU
Youdian Xincun
Dongshahonggang Lu
Xingang Lu
Tianbao Lu
Heping Park
Tianzhen Lu
Hongguan Lu
Shajing Branch
Jingdong Lu
Dongshahonggang Lu
Linping Beilu
Yangjiaban Lu
Xiangyanqiao Lu
Anqin Lu
Tianbao Lu
Shahong Lu
Huiamuqiao Lu
Tianbao Lu
Wuhua Lu
Hongzhen Beijie
Linping Lu
Shajinggang Lu
Tongzhou Lu
Gaoyang Lu
Hailun Lu
Haila'er Lu
Yuezhou Lu
Linping Road
Wuzhou Lu
Jintian Lu
ZHOUJIAZUI LU
Tongzhou Lu
Xinlian Lu
Shangqiu Lu
Dongyuhang Lu
Xi'an Lu
N
0
400 m
400 yds
L
M

Duolun Lu Cultural Street

TOP 25

HIGHLIGHTS

- Shikumen houses
- Shops selling antiques, art and period bric-a-brac
- Bustling modern Chinese character and colonial-period mansions
- Atmospheric cafés

TIP

- The proximity of Duolun Lu and Lu Xun Park to each other and their complementary character should add up to a decent day out in old Hongkou.

This restored pedestrian street of typical shikumen houses and pebble-dash villas was once the haunt of radical writers. Now it is lined with art galleries, shops, teahouses and terrace cafés.

Shopping Take Metro Line 3 to Dongbaoxing Road, turn right out of the station, then left onto Sichuan Beilu, and a five-minute walk brings you to Duolun Lu, where many of the shops specialize in collectibles. You can find antiques and knickknacks at No. 181 and collectible stones at No.189. Have a coffee among movie memorabilia at the Old Film Café (No. 123) or check out clocks at the Shanghai Nanjing Bells Collection Museum (No. 193) and chopsticks dating back to the Ming dynasty at the Shanghai Chopsticks Museum (No.191).

From left to right: Great Virtue Church; a statue of Charlie Chaplin at the Old Film Café; people strolling along Duolun Lu Cultural Street

Culture You can photograph the old brick doorways, the clock tower and the former Great Virtue Church (No. 59), with its intriguing mixture of Chinese and Western styles. The church now houses small craft shops, or you can check out the exhibitions in the Shanghai Duolun Museum of Modern Art.

Literary Connections Bronze statues dotted along the street commemorate the coterie of radical liberal and Communist writers who met here in the 1930s, and who, between them, created a new Chinese literature, far removed in spirit from the fossilized tropes of the past. The most famous of them, Lu Xun, had a profound influence on Chinese literature and is still revered today. You can find out more about him by visiting the museum in Lu Xun Park (▷ 86).

THE BASICS

K2

South of Lu Xun Park and south of Tian'ai Lu, branching west off Sichuan Beilu

Dongbaoxing Road

4, 9, 18, 21

Cafés and teahouses

Shanghai Duolun Museum of Modern Art

duolunart.com

27 Duolun Lu

6587 6902

Tue–Sun 10–6

Inexpensive

Lu Xun Park

TOP 25

HIGHLIGHTS

- Lu Xun's mausoleum and Memorial Hall
- Boating lake

TIP

- An excellent way to meet locals is to come along to the English Corner in Lu Xun Park that is held on Sunday mornings.

If you want a window on Shanghai life away from the city center, then try to get to Lu Xun Park, where local people come to find refuge and meet friends away from their crowded housing conditions.

Hongkou Hongkou is the area north of Suzhou Creek (the Wusong River). A large part was the former American Concession before it merged with the British Concession in 1863. The accepted date of its foundation is 1848, when a church mission was established here. Hongkou became home to many Japanese, earning the soubriquet of Little Tokyo. Here also was the Mixed Court (so called because iit was administered by a Chinese magistrate and a foreign assessor), the Russian post office and various risqué cabarets.

The boating lake (left); locals playing Chinese chess (right)

Lu Xun Lu Xun Park, originally laid out in 1905, has a large lake with rowing boats for hire in the summer. Shrubs and flowers attract butterflies, while the open-air setting draws amateur painters and opera singers. Every autumn there are chrysanthemum shows.

Above all, the park is best known for its long associations with the eminent writer Lu Xun, who lived in Hongkou from 1927 until his death in 1936. He is famous in China for *The True Story of Ah Q*, which lampoons the Chinese character. His house, at 9 Dalu Xinchun, Sanyin Lu, on a street just outside the park, is open to the public and illustrates what housing was like in the Japanese part of Shanghai. In the park there is a museum dedicated to his life, as well as his mausoleum and his likeness cast in bronze.

THE BASICS

- K–L1
- 146 Jiangwan Lu
- Daily 6am–6pm
- Snacks sold at stands
- Hongkou Football Stadium
- 18, 21
- None
- Free

Shopping

1933

This astonishing art deco, multi-level British-designed abattoir has been cleverly converted to house shops and restaurants. The shops are not so fascinating, but the concrete structure is ideal for photo ops.
K4 10 Shajing Lu 6501 1933 8.30am–10pm Hailun Rd

GUO CHUN XIANG CURIOSITY SHOP

Some of the objects in this cluttered little shop are antiques, but "collector's items" might be a better way to describe the curios, pop-culture items, Mao badges, toys and Chinese bric-a-brac from as recently as the 1960s.
K2 179–181 Duolun Lu 5696 3948 Dongbaoxing Road 17, 18, 19, 21, 70

HONGKOU PLAZA

capitamallsasia.com
This eight-story shopping, dining, entertainment and lifestyle complex is located right by the Hongkou Football Stadium; it offers shoppers unrivaled transportation links. Anchored by huge hypermarket Carrefour, it features a mix of international and Chinese brand stores, while dining options here range from quick snacks and fast food to high-end cuisine.
K1 388 Xijiang Wanlu 2601 9088 Daily 10–10 Hongkou Stadium 132, 139

Where to Eat

PRICES

Prices are approximate, based on a 3-course meal for one person.

$$$	more than 250RMB
$$	100–250RMB
$	under 100RMB

AFANTI RESTAURANT ($)

There are several excellent Uiguir/Muslim restaurants in town and this is one of the best. Don't be put off by the unimpressive interior because the food—largely grilled lamb—really hits the spot. When you have had enough Shanghai food, this is a great place for trying authentic naan bread, kebabs (*yangrouchuan*) and other varied cuisine from northwest China's Central Asian-Silk Road frontierland.
Off map Tianshan Hotel, 775 Quyang Lu 6555 9604 Daily 9am–10pm Chifeng Road

VUE BAR ($$$)

www.hyatt.com
One of the best bar experiences in town, Vue Bar in the Hyatt on the Bund has an outdoor terrace equipped with a jacuzzi, regular DJ sets and, most importantly, terrific views over to Lujiazui and the Bund to the south. There's an admission fee with one drink included, though you can also pair it with a visit to the Vue restaurant downstairs. Dress is smart/casual.
K5 32nd–33rd floor, Hyatt on the Bund, 199 Huangpu Lu 6393 1234 ext 6348 Sun–Wed 5.30pm–1.30am, Thu–Sat 5.30pm–2.30am Tiantong Rd

Pudong

Pudong is a city of 1.5 million people, typified by towering skyscrapers, nocturnal neon lights and vast avenues. The area sprang up from farmland inless than 20 years, soon becoming an icon of 21st-century China.

Top 25

5
6
7
8
9
J
K
BUND SIGHTSEEING TUNNEL
Shanghai Natural Wild Insect Kingdom
Shanghai International Convention Centre
Fenghe Lu
Oriental Pearl Tower
YAN'AN DONGLU TUNNEL
Lujiazui Xilu
Riverside Park
Super Brand Mall
PUDONG
Fucheng Lu
Shangri La Hotel
Lujiazui
Huanlu
LAN NI DU
RENMIN LU TUNNEL
Huangpu
FUXING DONGLU TUNNEL
N

Huangpu
XINJIAN LU TUNNEL
Binjiang
Dadao
Taidong
Lu
Mingzhu Park
Shanghai Ocean World Aquarium
Huanlu
Lujiazui
Lujiazui
LUJIAZUI
HUANLU
Yincheng Lu
Pudong Nanlu
Yincheng Zhonglu
Jimo
Lujiazui Green
Changyi Lu
Marine Tower
Mosque
Yincheng Zhonglu
Jin Mao Building
PUDONG DADAO
Pudong Skyscrapers
Lu
Huayuanshiqiao Lu
Shanghai World Financial Center
CENTURY AVENUE (SHIJI DADAO)
Zhaoyuan Lu
LUJIAZUI FINANCIAL AND TRADE ZONE
LUJIAZUI HUANLU
Qixia Lu
Dongchang Road
Xilu
Dongchang Lu
PUDONG NANLU
Laoshan
Rushan Lu
World Plaza
CENTURY AVENUE (SHIJI DADAO)
Puchang Lu
Shangcheng Lu
Shangcheng Road
Shangcheng Lu
Pumin Lu
Qixin Lu
ZHANGYANG LU
ZHANGYANG LU
Times Square
Qianjiaxiang Lu
PUDONG NANLU
0
400 m
0
400 yds
L
M

Oriental Pearl Tower

TOP 25

HIGHLIGHTS

- Spectacular views across the city
- A glimpse into the future of Shanghai

TIP

- There are several other places in Pudong where you can get similar views, including the world's second-highest observation deck at the Shanghai World Financial Center (▷ 94) or the 88th-floor observation deck of the Jinmao Tower (▷ 94).

The Oriental Pearl Tower rises as a 1990s monument to China's gravity-defying ambitions, and it offers fantastic views across Shanghai. It is emblematic of Lujiazui—the new-fangled forest of high-rises visible across the Huangpu River from the Bund.

Sky High Towering above the western end of Pudong is now the fastest-growing urban area in the world—the Oriental Pearl Tower is the third-tallest tower in Asia and the fifth-loftiest in the world (the world's second-tallest building, rather than tower, is the nearby Shanghai Tower, ▷ 94). Devoid of any natural grace and typical of the brash early 1990s that sent its concrete form skyward, the tower has nonetheless come to symbolize Shanghai.

Clockwise from left: The Pudong skyline and the Oriental Pearl Tower; illuminated stairs of the Oriental Pearl Tower; there are superb vistas from both viewing platforms

Visiting the Tower Most visitors are here for the views, but you'll need to weigh up the complicated ticketing system first to decide on what you want to see. There are a total of four observation floors, with the most expensive at the very top; the glass-floored observation platform at 850ft (259m) is not the highest, but is popular with those who like plunging, vertigo-inducing sensations. There's also a virtual-reality rollercoaster ride 322ft (98m) up and an interesting revolving restaurant.

The River A short walk away, the Riverside Promenade is an attractive counterpoint to the tower, with views alongside the Huangpu River across to the historic buildings of the Bund (▷ 58–59). Boat tours are available from the nearby dock situated to the north of the tower.

THE BASICS

orientalpearltower.com
- K6
- 1 Shiji Dadao (Century Avenue)
- 5879 1888
- Daily 8am–9.30pm
- Lujiazui
- Bund Sightseeing Tunnel
- Ferry from opposite Yan'an Donglu
- Moderate
- Moderate

Pudong Skyscrapers

TOP 25

Inside (left) and outside (right) the Jin Mao Tower

THE BASICS

Jin Mao Tower
jinmao88.com
L7
88 Shiji Dadao (Century Avenue)
5047 5101
Restaurants and cafés
Lujiazui
Free

Shanghai World Financial Center
swfc-observatory.com
L7
100 Shiji Dadao (Century Avenue)
Restaurants and cafés
Lujiazui
Free (charge for observation deck)

HIGHLIGHTS

- Views from the Jin Mao Tower's 88th-floor observation deck
- Views from the observation decks of the Shanghai Tower
- Grand Hyatt Hotel's restaurants

TIP

- Toast sundown with a drink from the outside terrace of Flair on the 58th floor of the Ritz-Carlton Shanghai (8 Shiji Dadao).

Pudong's financial district is Asia's fastest growing. Many of the 6,000-plus skyscrapers in Shangha crowd here. The effect is both dwarfing and dazzling, and there are ample opportunities to climb into the clouds for some excellent views.

Jin Mao Tower A Chinese pagoda inspired the design of this soaring edifice, now the 16th tallest in the world, at 1,380ft (420m). On clear days the 88th-floor observation deck gives spectacular views of Shanghai. You can send a postcard direct from the Post Office. After dark, enjoy views of the city's lights and the gourmet restaurants of the Grand Hyatt Hotel (▷ 112), occupying floors 53 through 87.

Shanghai World Financial Center Shaped like a bottle opener, this 1,614ft-high (492m) tower is the seventh-tallest building in the world. Completed in 2008, it is home to the Park Hyatt Shanghai (▷ 112) and three observation decks, on the 94th, 97th, and 100th floors (the latter is the second-highest observation deck in the world).

Shanghai Tower Opened in mid-2016, Shanghai's newest skyscraper is the second-tallest building in the world, and China's tallest, at 2,073ft (632m). The tower twists 120 degrees from base to tip and its 121 occupied floors include shops, offices, entertainment, a luxury hotel, cultural venues and the world's highest observation deck.

More to See

CENTURY PARK

centurypark.com.cn

Here you'll find a lake (where you can rent boats), gardens, pavilions and children's play areas.

Off map, east of M8 Huamu Lu and Jinxiu Lu 3876 0588 Daily 7–6 (until 5 mid-Nov to mid-Mar) Century Park Good Inexpensive

LUJIAZUI GREEN

This large, tree-fringed garden with a lake at its heart is popular with the workers of Pudong's offices.

L6 Lujiazui Lu 24 hours Lujiazui Good Free

SHANGHAI DISNEYLAND

www.shanghaidisneyresort.com

If you've kids in tow, this is an obvious choice, but be prepared to queue and brace yourself for some spectacular crowds. The TRON light-cycle power run and Pirates of the Caribbean are big attractions.

Off map (southeast of Pudong) 3158 0000 Daily 9am–9pm Disney Resort Good Expensive

SHANGHAI OCEAN WORLD AQUARIUM

sh-aquarium.com

It's the sharks, penguins and spider crabs that draw the crowds, but this is also a rare chance to see endangered Chinese species. A highlight is walking through the amazing glass underwater tunnel that is 509ft (155m) long.

L6 1388 Lujiazui Huanlu 5877 9988 Daily 9–6 (until 9 Jul and Aug); animal feeding times 9.45–11.10, 2.15–3.40 Lujiazui Few Expensive

SHANGHAI SCIENCE AND TECHNOLOGY MUSEUM

sstm.org.cn

This state-of-the-art museum is the largest of its kind in Asia. The scope of the exhibition extends from biodiversity and space exploration to design innovation and digital technology.

Off map at M8 2000 Shiji Dadao (Century Avenue) 6862 2000 Tue–Sun 9–5.15 Shanghai Science and Technology Museum Few Expensive

The beautiful flower beds at Century Park

Shopping

CHIA TAI DEPARTMENT STORE

This branch of the Thai department store chain, covering four floors of the Super Brand Mall, had a shaky start as shoppers were slow to take to Pudong as a retail center. That has changed now that the store stocks a broader range of goods and the parent mall has reached a wider audience.

K6 168 Lujiazui Lu 6887 7888 Daily 10–10 Lujiazui

WAL-MART SUPERCENTER

wal-martchina.com

This branch of the US chain store, one of ten in Shanghai, is at the south end of Pudong's main development zone, near the Nanpu Bridge approach road.

Off map at L9 252–262 Linyi Beilu 5094 5881 Daily 9am–10pm Tangqiao

YATAI XINYANG FASHION AND GIFT MARKET

This mall below the Metro station at the Shanghai Science and Technology Museum (▷ 95) sells modestly priced goods, from clothing to jewelry.

Off map at M9 2002 Shiji Dadao (Century Avenue) 6854 2269 Daily 10–7 Science and Technology Museum

SLOW START

Pudong has been slow to take off as a shopping district. This is because shoppers have been slow to change their habits. Now, as more people settle in Pudong, and as the effects of the generally high level of disposable income of people living and working in Pudong have kicked in, the picture is changing. Retailers, large and small, cheap and expensive, are moving in.

Where to Eat

PRICES

Prices are approximate, based on a 3-course meal for one person.

$$$	more than 250RMB
$$	100–250RMB
$	under 100RMB

JADE ON 36 ($$$)

shangri-la.com

This exceptional restaurant, on the 36th floor of the Shangri-La Hotel's stunning Tower Two, is a gem of intercontinental, multicultural fusion in a setting of modernist China themes. Views look out onto the Bund and to the city beyond, making it a tempting sunset choice.

K6 Pudong Shangri-La Hotel, 33 Fucheng Lu 6882 8888 Daily 10am–2pm, 5.30–10pm Lujiazui

ON 56 ($$$)

Located high up in the Grand Hyatt, here you can choose between fine Italian cuisine at Cucina, steaks and seafood at Grill or Japanese delights at Kobachi, with astonishing views coming as standard with every meal. The Sunday brunch is always a popular blow out and a further excuse to indulge, if you should need one.

L7 Grand Hyatt, Jin Mao Tower, 88 Shiji Dadao 5047 8838 Daily 11.30am–2.30pm & 5.30–10.30pm Lujiazui

Farther Afield

Other attractions lie a little bit farther from the heart of the city, but are still easy to reach and provide another dimension to a trip to Shanghai. With most sights busy on weekends, weekday trips are advised for eluding the crowds.

Top 25

Dachang
Taopu
5
20
Jiangqiao
2/42
ZHENROU
PUTUO
Jade Buddha Temple
Changfeng Park
Wusong
BEIXINJING
JINGAN
20
Hongqiao Airport
CHANGNING
Shanghai Zoo
SHANGHAI
XUHUI
Hongqiao
20
Expo Site
20
Shanghai South Station
320
Botanical Garden
Huangpu
ZHUHANG
20
4

Jiangwan
N
HONGKOU
ZHABEI
YANGPU
SHANGHAI
STATION
HUANGPU
Huangpu
LUWAN
NANSHI
PUDONG
110
Pudong
International
Airport
Beicai
Chuanyang He
YANGSI
Sanlin
Yuqiao
0
3 km
0
2 miles

Expo Site

TOP 25

HIGHLIGHTS

- Art collections
- Stunning architecture
- Shanghai Biennale art show

TIP

- Take a ferry to visit the Expo Site, so that you can enjoy views of Shanghai's burgeoning skyline along the way.

The 1,300-acre site for China's first world's fair, Expo 2010—attended by a record-breaking 73 million people over six months—has been left with several decent museums and arts and performance venues.

Museums and Performance Arenas The sprawling site is notable for several modern museums and cultural arenas: the former Expo Cultural Center where the opening ceremony was staged is now the Mercedes-Benz Arena, with an 18,000-seat auditorium hosting concerts by Chinese and international stars. Eight former Expo buildings have now become Chocolate Happy Land, a wacky theme park based around chocolate. There is also a riverside park.

Clockwise from top left: The 1km-long Expo Axis is a huge retail area; inside the business center in the Expo site; a spectacular video show on a screen above the entrance to the business center

THE BASICS

The 2010 Expo Site covers both sides of the Huangpu River, mostly in Pudong but also in Puxi.

China Art Museum

sh-artmuseum.org.cn

See map ▷ 99

205 Shangnan Lu

2025 2018

Tue–Sun 10–6, last entry 4pm

Café inside, restaurants and cafés nearby

China Art Museum

Good

Free; inexpensive for special exhibitions

Power Station of Art

powerstationofart.com

See map ▷ 99

200 Huayuangang Lu

3110 8550

Tue–Sun 11–7

Several restaurants and a café

South Xizang Road

65, 928

Good

Moderate for special exhibitions

China Art Museum The striking red building that was formerly the Expo's China Pavilion is the home for part of the collection from the now-closed Shanghai Art Museum in People's Square and is also known as the China Art Palace. Its five floors have permanent displays of 20th-century Chinese paintings, augmented by temporary exhibitions covering art, photography, stone carvings, historic art treasures and other themes.

Power Station of Art This former power station across the Huangpu River from the main Expo Site now pays homage to post-1980s art from China and around the world in its lofty interior, having been the Pavilion of the Future for the 2010 fair. Every two years it stages the Shanghai Biennale contemporary art exhibition previously held at the Shanghai Art Museum.

Jade Buddha Temple

TOP 25

HIGHLIGHTS

- Active temple
- Beautiful jade carvings

TIPS

- The temple is home to a famous vegetarian restaurant where you can enjoy tasty Chinese Buddhist meat-free dishes. As is the Buddhist way, food is prepared to resemble the texture of meat.
- Photographing either of the jade Buddha statues in the temple is not permitted.

Shanghai's most famous temple stands among high-rises in the city's north. The highlight of this small Buddhist shrine is its Jade Buddha in the library and the atmosphere of veneration and devotion.

The Temple The Jade Buddha Temple (Yufo Si) is one of Shanghai's few historic Buddhist temples. It was established in 1882 by a monk from the sacred mountain of Putuoshan (the home of the Buddhist Goddess of Mercy), in Zhejiang province, to house the jade figures. Abandoned after the fall of the Qing dynasty in 1911 and then restored between 1918 and 1928, the temple has endured the vicissitudes of the 20th century but has been well preserved. It is certainly not one of China's largest, but is an impressive example of the South

Clockwise from top left: Lighting candles from an open flame; a young woman raises a lighted candle; three Buddhas in the temple complex; dragon detail on the facade; a huge incense burner in the courtyard

Chinese style, especially the roof of the main hall, with its steeply raised eaves and decorative figurines. The temple is particularly worth visiting on the first and fifth days of each month, holy days that attract many worshipers.

The Jade Buddhas The temple has several halls, including the impressive Hall of Heavenly Kings and the ornate Great Treasure Hall, with its three golden Buddhas. The highlights, however, are the two jade statues brought from Burma by Abbott Wei Ken, both carved from a single piece of creamy jade and separately housed. The first is a 3ft-long (1m) reclining Buddha. The more beautiful figure is the one in the library; almost 6.5ft (2m) high, it weighs around 2,200 lb (1,000kg), is encrusted with semi-precious stones and emits a divine aura.

THE BASICS

D3

170 Anyuan Lu, Putuo

6266 3668

Daily 8–5

Excellent vegetarian restaurant

Changshou Road

None

Inexpensive

Regular services

Shanghai Zoo

TOP 25

Residents of the zoo include birds of prey and red pandas

THE BASICS

shanghaizoo.cn
See map ▷ 98
Hongqiao, Hongqiao Lu (near airport)
Daily, Mar–Oct 7.30–5; Nov–Feb 7.30–4.30
Restaurants
Shanghai Zoo
57, 91, 519, 709, 748, 806, 807, 809, 911, 925, 936, 941
Few
Moderate

HIGHLIGHTS

- Giant pandas
- Polar bears
- Green lawns
- Play areas for children

In addition to its collection of creatures, Shanghai Zoo is one of the city's most pleasant expanses of greenery and parkland, making it a perfect day out.

Green Space This is one of the few parts of Shanghai where you can lie down on the grass in the sun with a soft drink. There's more of a sense of parkland here than at many other of Shanghai's more synthetic "parks." This is a fun and educational place for children and there are play areas scattered around, as well as a children's zoo. Unfortunately, living quarters for the animals are not the best. The authorities are constantly making improvements, but overall the zoo can hardly rank with large city zoos in Europe or the US. However, the zoo does cooperate with international schemes to preserve rare and endangered species.

Panda Stars Needless to say, the giant and lesser pandas are the stars of the show, and their compound is the best laid-out, covering a large part of the 183 acre (74ha) zoo. It has an indoor and an outdoor area, with a rockery, a pond and trees. But there is much more to the zoo, with some 620 species in total, ranging in size from butterflies to Asian elephants, with animals from all continents. Among them are Brazilian wolves, African chimpanzees, penguins, peacocks, tigers, koalas, a polar bear, golden-haired and squirrel monkeys, gorillas, South American buffalo and Père David's (Milu) deer.

Excursions

HANGZHOU

Within easy reach of Shanghai, Hangzhou is one of China's top tourist destinations and a historic former capital city, renowned for its magnificent West Lake.

Hangzhou's prosperity came from the Grand Canal, which linked south and north China, but the city was also the capital of the Southern Song dynasty. Today it is a green and attractive city. Most of Hangzhou's sights cluster around the West Lake just west of the center. Jump on a rental bicycle and circumnavigate the lake; starting at the Mausoleum of Yue Fei and cycling eastward, you'll pass Gushan Island, the Baochu Pagoda (overlooking West Lake from the hills to the north), then cycle south to the Leifeng Pagoda and the Jingci Temple and return via the Su Causeway through the lake itself. You can also take a boat trip to Xiaoying Island and the Mid-Lake Pavilion.

Off in the west is Hangzhou's most famous temple, the magnificent Lingyin Temple, one of Buddhist China's most important shrines. Hangzhou's museums are all free. Make sure you visit the China Silk Museum (in Yuhuangshan Lu) and the China Tea Museum (in Longjing Lu).

THE BASICS

Distance: 105 miles (170km)

Many restaurants and cafés

Fast trains run to Hangzhou in around 80 minutes from Shanghai South Railway Station

Few facilities

Stay overnight to make the most of your visit. Hotels range from the luxurious Grand Hyatt Regency (28 Hubin Lu, tel 0571-8779 1234) to a strong selection of budget and mid-range choices not far from the city center. Another highlight of Hangzhou is its excellent choice of restaurants, many within strolling distance of West Lake.

SHE SHAN

She Shan is a hill with an imposing redbrick Catholic church known as "Our Lady of China" at the summit. Mass continues to be celebrated here in Latin.

Its origins go back to the mid-19th century, when a wave of xenophobia led to the construction of a small chapel on the remote hillside. An acting bishop of Shanghai, later forced to take refuge here, vowed that in return for protection he would build a church (the current one dates from 1925). May is the busiest time for pilgrimages, when streams of people climb the hill paths, which represent the Via Dolorosa (the route Jesus took to his crucifixion). Next to the church is a small observatory, one of China's oldest.

THE BASICS

Distance: 19 miles (30km); 6 miles (10km) north of Songjiang town

Train from Guilin Road station (on Metro line 9) direct to She Shan station

Church

5765 1521

Daily 9–5

Restaurants and cafés nearby

Free

THE BASICS

Distance: 62 miles (100km)

Restaurants and cafés

Regular fast trains take less than 30 minutes to reach Suzhou from Shanghai Railway Station

Few facilities

Bicycles can be rented at the Mingtown Youth Hostel (28 Pingjiang Lu, tel 0512 6581 6869) and at any other hostel

SUZHOU

Suzhou is one of China's best-known canal towns and its gardens are famed all across the land.

The Garden of the Master of the Nets (off Shiquan Jie, in the south of town) shows how a compact space can give the illusion of size; the Humble Administrator's Garden (178 Dongbei Jie, in the north of town) is a far larger garden.

Suzhou also has some fine temples and pagodas, including the West Garden Temple (Xiyuan Lu), the North Temple Pagoda (Renmin Lu), the Twin Pagodas, the Temple of Mystery (Guanqian Jie) and the Hanshan Temple. The Ruiguang Pagoda, near the Grand Canal in the south of Suzhou, rises up alongside Pan Gate (also called Panmen Gate), part of the original city wall.

Suzhou's museums are also excellent. Suzhou Museum (204 Dongbei Jie), designed by I.M. Pei, is visually stunning. Also worth visiting are the Suzhou Silk Museum (2001 Renmin Lu) and the Kunqu Opera Museum (14 Zhongzhangjia Xiang). If you want to spend the night, there are various options, from youth hostels to five-star hotels.

THE BASICS

Distance: 19 miles (30km)

Restaurants and cafés

Regular buses to Zhujiajiao run from Pu'an Road Bus Station just south of People's Square in the center of Shanghai

ZHUJIAJIAO

Zhujiajiao is a small canal town with a wealth of historic features and archetypal images of traditional China.

Although the settlement is much older, it wasn't until the Ming dynasty that Zhujiajiao emerged as a prosperous and well-to-do canal town. Much of the Ming and Qing dynasty layout and architecture survives in the old town and a leisurely meander round its alleys turns up countless surprises. There are several old bridges but the standout sight is the long, hump-backed span of the Fangsheng Bridge, which dates from the 16th century.

The Yuanjin Buddhist Temple is worth hunting down, as is the Catholic Church of Ascension, dating to the mid-19th century. You can also take boat tours along the canal.

Shanghai has a superb choice of places to stay, from glittering five-star towers to crisply efficient business hotels, boutique hideaways, low-cost chain hotels and a growing band of affordable lodgings for the more budget-conscious.

Introduction

Shanghai is top-heavy with high-end hotels on the Huangpu River, but mid-range and budget options are also expanding.

Variety of Accommodations

Hotels with historic character are plentiful but some may lack international finesse. There is a glut of five-star hotels of international quality and a growing band of intimate, fashionable boutique hotels. The English-language skills of staff are generally satisfactory at five-star hotels, but can be lacking even in four-star establishments; staff attitudes can still be problematic in locally managed hotels where the nuances of international service may not be apparent. There's a mushrooming band of well-located youth hostels, which tend to have young and fluent English-speaking staff and inexpensive but comfortable double rooms.

Location

The most fashionable areas are around the Bund, Nanjing Lu, People's Square and the French Concession. Pudong is awash with high-end hotels, but—apart from the excellent views from high-rise hotels—there's little charm.

Room Prices

Prices can be steep so reserve beforehand for the best deals. The official rack rate is rarely levied, beyond peak periods such as the May 1 and October 1 holidays.

STARS IN THEIR COURSES

The hotel star-rating system employed in China can often be a reliable guide to what you can expect from a hotel, but not always, and may even be misleading in some cases. The nationally determined five-star category generally means what it says, though many hotels that are a decade or two old have never seen any modernization or upgrading, or even a lick of paint, since they were built. Four- and three-star hotels might have been "assisted" to their status by a "sympathetic" local official. Two- and one-star hotels can be surprisingly dowdy and may even have safety issues.

From top: The Face Bar at the InterContinental Shanghai Ruijin; Orient Hotel; colonial detail; Fairmont Peace Hotel

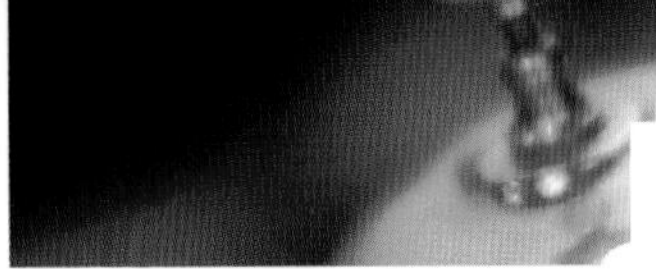

Budget Hotels

PRICES

Expect to pay under 700RMB for a double room per night for a budget hotel.

EAST ASIA HOTEL

jinjianginns.com

In a historic building on Nanjing Donglu, the East Asia Hotel has long been a decent budget standby in the best part of the city. The area can be noisy—this is Nanjing Donglu after all—but you are right at the heart of the action. Check rooms first as some are noisier than others, depending on which direction they face.

H5 680 Nanjing Donglu 6322 3223 Nanjing Road (E)

FISH INN

fishinn.com.cn

Boutique hotel with 30 rooms in a traditional shikumen area next to Suzhou Creek and near to Nanjing Lu's shops and the Bund. Don't expect too many niceties but the rooms are clean and each has a traditional theme.

J5 639 Henan Zhonglu 6324 2210 Nanjing Road (E)

HOME INN

homeinns.com

This branch enjoys a decent location near the Bund as well as a more traditional alleyway setting. It's not the most comfortable choice, but it's clean and makes for a dependable, if rather utilitarian, stay at the heart of town.

J6 Lane 26, Sijing Road 6323 9966 East Nanjing Road

MOTEL 168

motel168.com

If you're looking for a clean and modern hotel aimed at the lower end of the Chinese business market, chain hotel Motel 168 is excellent value.

Off map 1119 West Yan'an Lu 5118 0999 Jiangsu Road

PARK HOTEL

internationalshotel.com

The Park Hotel is a classic prewar skyscraper, though modernized a little garishly. It has an excellent location and facilities, which include a business area, shopping arcade, beauty salon and several good restaurants.

G5 170 Nanjing Xilu 5180 1133 People's Park/People's Square 20, 37

SEVENTH HEAVEN

7hotel.cn

In a distinctive prewar building on Nanjing Lu, Seventh Heaven has reasonable prices. Rooms are fairly well equipped and facilities include a business center, post office and Cantonese and Sichuan restaurants.

H5 627 Nanjing Donglu 6322 0777 People's Square 37

YUEYANG HOTEL

This long-standing French Concession hotel is a decent and dependable choice, with spacious rooms, although rather basic English can be spoken. The location is excellent, just a short walk from the Metro system.

C8 58 Yueyang Lu 6466 6767 Hengshan Road

RESERVATIONS

If you are on a tight budget, it is best not to arrive in Shanghai without a hotel reservation. Budget accommodations are in fairly short supply, and wandering about this huge city with luggage could prove time consuming, expensive and very tiring.

Mid-Range Hotels

PRICES

Expect to pay between 700 and 1,500RMB for a double room per night for a mid-range hotel.

BROADWAY MANSIONS HOTEL

broadwaymansions.com

Renovated with a crisp new interior, this art deco hotel has a fantastic position, with views of the Huangpu River and Lujiazui, while overlooking Suzhou Creek and Waibaidu Bridge.

K5 20 Suzhou Beilu 6324 6260 Tiantong Road

CENTRAL HOTEL

This popular hotel is all about good value and a location almost right on Nanjing Lu, a short walk from both the Bund and People's Square. It's difficult to get more central than this.

H5 555 Jiujiang Lu 5396 5000 Nanjing Road (E)

CYPRESS HOTEL JIN JIANG

jin-jiang-cypress.theshanghaihotels.com

About 1 mile (2km) from Hongqiao Airport and with a free shuttle bus to the city center, this modern hotel is set in gardens that give a sense of being in the country; you can even fish in a lake. Rooms are functional but attractive.

Off map 2419 Hongqiao Lu 6268 8868 91, 911, 925

HENGSHAN PICARDIE HOTEL

hengshanhotel.com

Restorations have brought a measure of class back to this art deco hotel—once the Picardie Apartments—on the French Concession edges. Excellent discounts are a further bonus.

B8 534 Hengshan Lu 6437 7050 Hengshan Road

HOTEL EQUATORIAL

equatorial.com

This high-rise hotel, not far from the western part of Nanjing Lu, has a steak-house, Italian, Cantonese and Japanese restaurants, and a 24-hour café. There's also a gym, pool, sauna and tennis and squash courts; service is polite and efficient and rooms offer comfort and value for money.

C6 65 Yan'an Xilu 6248 1688 Jing'an Temple 57, 925

HOWARD JOHNSON HUAIHAI HOTEL SHANGHAI

A comfortable hotel in the heart of the French Concession with shops and restaurants a short stroll away—which makes up for the fact that the rooms are now a bit tired and service can be somewhat lacking.

D7 1 Fenyang Lu 5461 9898 Shanxi Road (S)

HYATT ON THE BUND

hyattonthebund.cn

It's not quite on the Bund, but the Hyatt's two towers have great views of the Bund and Pudong. The modern decor is stylish without going overboard, and rooms are spacious and cutting-edge.

K5 199 Huangpu Lu 6393 1234 Tiantong Road

INTERCONTINENTAL SHANGHAI RUIJIN

ihg.com

Guests stay in five redbrick villas—mostly dating from the 1920s—in the grounds of the former Morris Estate. The setting is simply stunning: Within a walled enclosure are a Japanese garden, a small lake and manicured lawns. The tasteful rooms are a good size, and

some have balconies overlooking the pretty garden.
E8 118 Ruijin 2-Lu 6472 5222 Shanxi Road (S)

JIN JIANG HOTEL

This art deco French Concession hotel is just off Huaihai Zhonglu, so sightseeing and shopping are a breeze. Rooms are in various buildings, with very different tariffs. There are excellent restaurants.
E7 59 Maoming Nanlu 3218 9888 Shanxi Road (S)

KEVIN'S OLD HOUSE

This lovely place only has six suites, but it's a winning choice if you want to spend the night in a charming, historical French Concession villa, with all the flavor of yesteryear, even including wooden floorboards.
C6 No. 4, Lane 946, Changle Road 6248 6800 Changshu Road

MARRIOTT HONGQIAO

marriott.com/shaqi

This family-friendly hotel offers excellent facilities at reasonable prices. While handy for Hongqiao Airport, it is also close to the Yan'an Expressway, with its fast transit to the center. Rooms are spacious and tastefully furnished, and there's a gym and sauna to enjoy after a day of sightseeing.
Off map 2270 Hongqiao Lu 6010 6000 Shanghai Zoo

NEW WORLD MAYFAIR HOTEL

shanghai.newworldhotels.com

Efficient and neat, this business hotel offers views from its north side over Zhongshan Park. Although located in the west of the city, it's next to Zhongshan Park Metro station for swift access to town on line 2.
Off map 1555 Dingxi Lu 6240 8888 Zhongshan Park

NOVOTEL ATLANTIS

novotel.com

While it mimics the typical model of a large, business-oriented tower hotel, its ownership by a French chain affords the Atlantis some refreshing design and service touches. It's a bit isolated, but its four restaurants, three bars, pool and other amenities compensate.
Off map 728 Pudong Dadao 5036 6666 Pudong Avenue

RADISSON BLU HOTEL SHANGHAI NEW WORLD

radisson.com/shanghaicn_newworld

Rising over People's Park and People's Square, this modern tower—topped with a flying-saucer-style revolving restaurant—offers excellent value, first-rate views and a host of facilities, plus a high-altitude bar.
G5 88 Nanjing Xilu 6359 9999 People's Square

TAIYUAN VILLA

ruijinhotelsh.com

This elegant and comfortable French-Renaissance-style mansion is set in a secluded garden. Most accommodations are in villas around the mansion. The hotel has few facilities, but there are plenty of bars and restaurants nearby.
D8 160 Taiyuan Lu 6471 6688 Hengshan Road

LODGING IN PUDONG

Pudong has a virtually complete absence of anything that resembles traditional Chinese style. But it is full of the brand new, making Pudong attractive in its own right, and it's easy enough to be whisked across the river.

Luxury Hotels

PRICES

Expect to pay more than 1,500RMB per night for a double room.

FAIRMONT PEACE HOTEL

fairmont.com

This art deco treasure (▷ 62) has been reinvented to cater for 21st-century visitors, with all the amenities and service you'd expect from one of Shanghai's premier hotels. Its legendary jazz band plays nightly from 7pm in the bar.

J5 20 Nanjing Donglu 6321 6888 Nanjing Road (E) 27

GRAND HYATT

shanghai.grand.hyatt.com

Spectacular views are the preserve of the Hyatt, which takes the top 34 floors of the Jin Mao Tower (▷ 94). All rooms have floor-to-ceiling windows, but those facing the river are most sought-after.

L7 88 Shiji Dadao (Century Avenue) 5049 1234 Lujiazui

OKURA GARDEN HOTEL SHANGHAI

gardenhotelshanghai.com

Close to Huaihai Zhonglu, this tower hotel sits behind the facade of the old French Club. It has five restaurants, including a Japanese one, a business area and health club. The south-facing rooms have lovely views over the lawn.

E7 58 Maoming Nanlu 6415 1111 Shanxi Road (S) 41

PARK HYATT

park.hyatt.com

Ranging over 15 floors of the Shanghai World Financial Center (▷ 94), the stylishly understated Park Hyatt is a serious good-looker, with luxurious, ultra-modern rooms and some astonishing views.

L7 100 Shiji Dadao (Century Avenue) 6888 1234 Lujiazui

THE PENINSULA SHANGHAI

shanghai.peninsula.com

This opulent hotel was the first new building on the Bund for seven decades and it capitalizes on its prime position with a rooftop terrace (▷ 65). Rooms come with lovely views; take the rear door to reach Yuanmingyuan Road.

J5 32 Zhongshan Dong 1-Lu 2327 2888 Nanjing Road (E) 65, 928

PORTMAN RITZ-CARLTON

ritzcarlton.com

This hotel—an intrinsic part of the Shanghai Centre—is one of the most superior business hotels in Shanghai, in one of the best parts of town. Service, facilities and rooms are all top-notch and the overall presentation is excellent.

D5 1376 Nanjing Xilu 6279 8888 Jing'an Temple 20, 37

RITZ-CARLTON SHANGHAI PUDONG

ritzcarlton.com

The rooms in this standout Pudong hotel are stylistically delightful and an indulgent pleasure, while standards of service are effortlessly high and the outside terrace of the signature bar, Flair, is a must-do nighttime experience.

K6 Shanghai IFC, Shiji Dadao 2020 1888 Lujiazui

HOTEL SERVICE

Hotel staff will write down your destination in Chinese for you to show to taxi drivers. Ask the doorman to make sure the driver knows exactly where you want to go—and don't forget to take the hotel's own name-card with you for the return journey.

Use this section to help you plan your visit to Shanghai. We have suggested the best ways to get around the city and useful information for when you are there.

Planning Ahead

When to Go

The best time to visit Shanghai is either in late spring (April/May) or in early fall (late September to October), when days can be clear and warm and comfortable for exploring on foot. June and July are very hot and see occasional epic rainstorms; August is also very hot. Winter is miserable, damp and cold.

TIME

Shanghai is 13 hours ahead of New York and 8 hours ahead of the UK. Shanghai does not have daylight saving.

AVERAGE DAILY MAXIMUM TEMPERATURES

JAN	FEB	MAR	APR	MAY	JUN	JUL	AUG	SEP	OCT	NOV	DEC
45°F	46°F	50°F	64°F	73°F	79°F	88°F	86°F	77°F	72°F	61°F	50°F
7°C	8°C	10°C	18°C	23°C	26°C	31°C	30°C	25°C	22°C	16°C	10°C

Spring (March to May) is a pleasant time. The trees begin to blossom in April; May is usually comfortably warm but is often wet.
Summer (June to August) is extremely hot and humid, particularly July and August.
Fall (September to October) is often pleasantly warm, although September is also one of the wetter months, and watch out for unexpectedly hot days.
Winter (November to February) is cold, clammy and overcast with occasional snow, but temperatures don't often fall below freezing. It can be an unpleasant time to be in Shanghai.

WHAT'S ON

The dates of traditional Chinese festivals vary from year to year according to the lunar calendar, which usually begins in February.

Winter/spring *Chinese New Year/Spring Festival*: The most important festival in the Chinese calendar usually falls in February. Red envelopes containing money are given to encourage prosperity. It's a festive time to be in the city, but getting tickets for journeys out of town can be tricky.
Lantern Festival (15th day of the first lunar month): Locals eat *tangyuan* (sticky and sweet dumplings), visit temples and may hang out paper lanterns.
Guanyin's Birthday (19th day of the second moon): Guanyin is the goddess of mercy, and on her birthday Buddhist temples are filled with worshipers.
Longhua Temple Fair (third lunar month): Celebrating the founding of Longhua Temple.
May *International Labor Day* (May 1): Three-day holiday.
Music Festival: A festival of classical western and traditional music.
June *Children's Day* (Jun 1).
September *Mid-Autumn Festival* (15th day of the eighth moon): Recalls a 14th-century uprising against the Mongols and is now celebrated with Moon cakes, filled with lotus root, dates and sesame.
October *National Day* (Oct 1): Celebration of the founding of the People's Republic of China. Week-long holiday.
November *Shanghai Marathon*.
December *Christmas Day* (Dec 25): Increasingly a festive event in Shanghai.

Shanghai Online

shine.cn/news
The English online version of the *Shanghai Daily* presents a somewhat sober style and all the news the government thinks is fit to print. But it contains plenty of useful news, views and information about practical matters.

timeoutshanghai.com
Exhaustive details about forthcoming Shanghai events as well as readable and extensive listings for restaurants, bars, clubs, art galleries and attractions.

shanghaiist.com
One of the city's best general websites, aimed mainly at the young, footloose, fancy-free and ready-to-party.

smartshanghai.com
This hip site aims to get you to the coolest parties, raves, dance clubs and other venues where the action is hot and happening.

travelchinaguide.com
This comprehensive general China travel website covers cultural issues in Shanghai in reasonable depth, providing decent introductions to places of interest and practical matters. Note that some information is dated.

thatsmags.com
That's Shanghai has bars, dining and entertainment listings as well as Shanghai features.

shanghaihighlights.com
The Shanghai website of tour operator China Highlights. It features many guided-tour and excursion options in the city.

shanghai.gov.cn
The official website of the Shanghai Municipality has an extensive English section covering city news and services, travel, leisure and hotels.

TRAVEL SITE

fodors.com
A complete travel-planning site. You can research prices and weather; book air tickets, cars and rooms; pose questions to fellow travelers; and find links to other sites.

WIFI

Hotels, restaurants and coffee shops in Shanghai are WiFi enabled. Remember that China polices the Internet in a draconian fashion, both to stifle opinion and to give domestic social media platforms and search engines enough room to flourish without competition: Facebook, Instagram, Twitter, Google, YouTube, Snapchat, Pinterest, Tumblr and Google Maps are all blocked and inaccessible, while news wires and newspapers can sometimes also be inaccessible. You can get around this by using a VPN (Virtual Private Network), though the authorities regularly threaten to crack down on their use.

Getting There

AIRPORT TAX

- 50RMB for domestic flights, 90RMB for international flights. These taxes are included in the price of air tickets.

ENTRY REQUIREMENTS

- Visitors must hold a valid passport with at least six months' validity.
- Visas for all foreign nationals must be obtained in advance from the nearest Chinese Consulate or Embassy. Tourist visas are generally valid for 30 days but can sometimes be extended in China. A visa-free stay in Shanghai for up to 144 hours is available to citizens of many countries providing they have onward tickets and visas to a third country.
- In Shanghai, visa extensions are issued by the Public Security Bureau ✉ 1500 Minsheng Lu, Pudong.
- No vaccinations are required unless you are coming from a yellow fever infected area. However, doctors may recommend certain precautionary measures.

AIRPORTS

International flights arrive at Shanghai Pudong International Airport (PVG), 19 miles (30km) east of the city. Domestic flights use Pudong International Airport or Hongqiao International Airport, in the west of Shanghai.

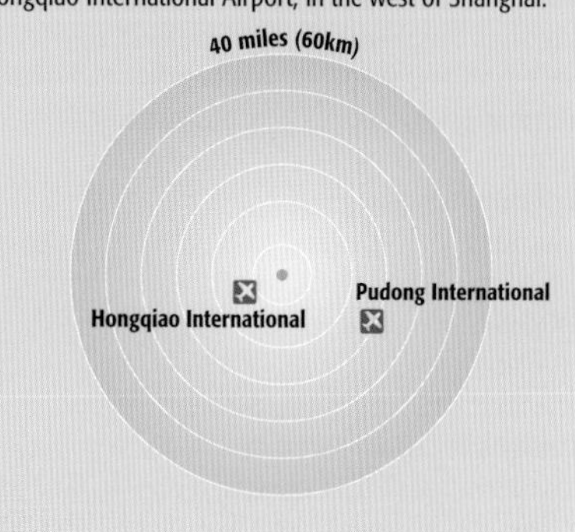

ARRIVING BY AIR (INTERNATIONAL)

The website for Shanghai Pudong International Airport is shanghaiairport.com. At the airport, information counters are by the domestic and international security check areas and airside in the domestic departure area. There is a luggage storage facility in International Arrivals (tel 96990, open daily 6am–11pm), as well as ATMs. The airport has a long-distance bus station for buses to Suzhou and Hangzhou. Transportation to Shanghai is by shuttle buses, taxi or Maglev, the world's first commercial Magnetic Levitation rail system. Shuttle buses leave every 10 to 30 minutes from Arrivals; the journey to central Shanghai takes from 40 minutes to an hour or more (seven routes). Buy tickets on the bus. Taxi stands are to the right outside the Arrivals hall. Have your destination written in Chinese, and ensure the meter is switched on. Ignore the unofficial taxi touts in and just outside the Arrivals hall. A taxi trip will take 30–60 minutes, depending on traffic and your destination. Maglev trains traveling at up to 267mph (430kph) take less than 8 minutes to reach Longyang Road Metro station, on Metro Line 2. Maglev is accessed via level 2.

ARRIVING BY AIR (DOMESTIC)

For information about arriving at Pudong International Airport, ▷ opposite. Some domestic flights arrive at the older and far less efficient Hongqiao Airport, in the western suburbs. Both Arrivals halls at Hongqiao have hotel shuttle desks, and outside the halls are bus stops for buses to Shanghai Railway Station, Shanghai Stadium, People's Square, Pudong International Airport and other points. Taxis take 30–40 minutes to travel to the city center.

ARRIVING BY BOAT

Two companies operate services from Japan: The Shanghai International Ferry Company, a weekly service from Osaka; and the China–Japan International Ferry Co., a weekly service from Kobe and/or Osaka. Crossings take two days; ships dock at the International Passenger Terminal in Hongkou.

Most domestic passengers arriving by boat do so on ferries from destinations on the East China Sea (Putuoshan) and the Yangtze River (Wuhan, Chongqing). These dock at the Wusong Passenger Terminal in the north of Shanghai or at Luchaogang in the south.

ARRIVING BY TRAIN

Most trains arrive at either Shanghai Hongqiao Train Station, Shanghai Train Station or Shanghai South Train Station. Hold onto your ticket until you are out of the terminal. Taxis are readily available or you can hop on the Metro from each station. If you don't have much luggage, the Metro is better than taking a taxi, especially if you have a long journey. Resist the temptation to find a hotel near any of the stations as they are generally in unappealing areas and you won't want to hang around. It's easiest to try to book any outward train tickets through your hotel, for a small service charge, but remember to book days ahead, especially for sleeper trains on popular routes. Getting hold of train tickets during the Chinese New Year, the May 1 and October 1 holiday periods can be tricky.

CUSTOMS REGULATIONS

- You may import 400 cigarettes, 1.5 liters of alcohol, 0.5 liters of perfume.
- When departing, be careful that any antique you have purchased is permitted to leave the country. Antiques that are permitted for export must bear a red seal and any item not carrying the seal may be seized at customs.

VISITORS WITH DISABILITIES

China is not a country that has made many concessions to people with disabilities. However, very slowly, things are improving. As new hotels and museums are constructed, so access is being made easier for wheelchair users and wheelchairs are more readily available at airports. However, attitudes, in general, are not thoughtful or considerate—you should be prepared for difficulties and for the need to improvise.

INSURANCE

- Travel insurance covering medical expenses is essential.
- In the event of medical treatment, be sure to keep all receipts.

Getting Around

MAPS

Tourist maps of Shanghai are widely available from bookshops, hotels and tourist information centers.

WALKING BLUES

While getting around on foot is a great way to see the city, remember that distances are large and the streets are filled with pedestrians, traffic and noise. It can be exhausting, particularly in summer. It makes more sense to go by taxi or public transportation to the general area you want to explore and walk from there. Be cautious at all times when crossing roads, even at traffic lights. Shanghai's drivers show no mercy to mere pedestrians.

TAXI TRIALS

Many taxi drivers have only a superficial knowledge of Shanghai's roads. Look at the number of stars below the driver's photo on the dashboard; one is a beginner, five is an expert. Very few drivers speak English well, so have the address of your destination written down in Chinese. Avoid illegal taxis. Well-known taxi companies include Dazhong Taxi (☎ 96822) and Qiangsheng Taxi (☎ 6258 0000).

BICYCLES

- Bicycles (*zixing che*) are widely used and can be rented at little cost from some hotels or from specialist outlets. Bicycles are banned from some large roads in Shanghai, however.
- Check brakes and tires before setting out and observe how traffic functions in China—joining it unprepared can be an unnerving experience.

BUSES

- The comprehensive bus system is very inexpensive but buses can be crowded, especially during rush hour; buses are not foreigner-friendly, unless you can read Chinese.
- Buses run between 5am and 11pm.
- The best buses are the hop-on hop-off tourist buses. City Sightseeing Buses and Big Bus Tours are the two companies that cover Shanghai's most popular areas, including the Bund, the Old Town, People's Square and the Jade Buddha Temple. Tickets are valid for either 24 hours or 48 hours.
- Make sure that you have small change—you pay your fare on board.
- Note that pushing your way on board is a feature of daily life. Pickpockets are a risk.

FERRIES

- Ferries cross the Huangpu River between Pudong and the Bund from 7am to 10pm. Single fares are 2RMB.

METRO

- Shanghai's Metro network (shmetro.com) currently has 14 lines, and is the longest Metro system in China at more than 400 miles (644km). The network is still ambitiously expanding, with plans to integrate the Shanghai Metro with the Metro system of Suzhou.
- The busiest station is People's Square, intersected by Lines 1, 2 and 8. Line 1 runs from Fujin Road in the north to Xinzhuang, via Shanghai Railway Station. Line 2 goes east from East Xujing Road to Pudong International Airport, via the Maglev station at Longyang

Road. Line 3 links North Jiangyang Road with Shanghai South Railway Station. Line 4 runs in a huge loop, linking Puxi and Pudong. Another useful line is Line 8, which runs from Yaohua Road in Pudong through People's Square to Shiguang Road.

- Trains run every few minutes from 5.30 or 6 in the morning until 10.30 or 11 in the evening, and platform screens show the next two trains due. Signs and announcements are in English and Chinese.
- Fares range from 3RMB to 15RMB. Travel in the central area on Lines 1 and 2 costs from 3RMB to 4RMB. Single tickets can be bought from station concourse vending machines or at ticket windows. For multiple journeys, buy a Shanghai Public Transportation Card, an electronic smart card swiped on automated ticket barriers. Refundable cards costing 20RMB are available from stations and convenience stores and can be topped up as desired. The cards can also be used for buses, taxis, ferries and the Maglev airport shuttle bus.
- Overcrowding is a problem during rush hour. Glass safety screens with sliding doors have been installed on some platform edges.
- Metro lines are being renamed. Each line number will be prefixed by a letter identifying it as an elevated light railway (L), a central business district subway (M) or suburbs (R).

TAXIS

- Taxis are widely available, metered and easy to flag down.
- Travel by taxi is quite inexpensive and a good way to get around, especially to areas not reached by the Metro.
- In general, Shanghai taxi drivers are very honest. However, if you are dissatisfied take note of the license number displayed inside and keep your receipt.
- Never accept an offer of a ride from a driver of an illegal taxi. There are plenty of legal taxis in the city.

RETURN ADDRESS

Always carry a card or handwritten note in Chinese stating your hotel name and address, and perhaps directions for how to get there if it is not likely to be well known or in an easily identifiable location. This will be particularly useful for taxi drivers—but might also come in handy if you have an accident or lose your wallet or purse. You could also carry information in Chinese about any chronic medical condition you have or any medicines you need to take.

SIDE TRIPS

Shanghai is near enough to several of China's most interesting small—by Chinese standards—cities: Suzhou (▷ 106; the city of classic Chinese gardens); Hangzhou (▷ 105; described by Marco Polo as paradise on earth); Nanjing (the former Ming dynasty and Republican capital as well as capital of the Taiping Kingdom on the Yangtze River, with historical tombs and some excellent museums); and Wuxi (the most convenient gateway to Lake Tai/Taihu). All of these can be reached by organized tour, or by train from Shanghai.

Essential Facts

EMERGENCY NUMBERS

- Ambulance ☎ 120
- Fire ☎ 119
- Police ☎ 110

MONEY

RMB (Renminbi) is the currency of China. The basic unit is the yuan (often called "kuai" in spoken Chinese), made up of 10 jiao (often called "mao" in spoken Chinese), each of which is divided into 10 fen (rarely used). There are notes for 1, 2, 5, 10, 20, 50 and 100 yuan, and the smaller 1, 2 and 5 jiao. There are also coins for 1 yuan; 1 and 5 jiao; and 5 fen.

ELECTRICITY

- The power supply is 220V, 50 cycles AC.
- Plug types vary, the most common is the two-flat-pin type. It is worth taking an adaptor.

ETIQUETTE

- Avoid displays of anger and aggression. If you have a complaint, gentle, persistent questioning is the best way of dealing with it.
- Remember that China is an authoritarian country where any contrary opinions are still actively discouraged.
- Table etiquette depends on where you eat. Good table manners are essential in smart restaurants, and especially at banquets, but at cheaper restaurants chicken bones are flung on the floor and loud-talking diners outdo each other to be heard.

MEDICAL TREATMENT

- Treatment is available in state hospitals and in private, joint-venture clinics.
- For minor ailments, the foreigner section of the state-run hospitals will normally be the cheapest option. However, try to ascertain the cost of treatment in advance.
- Your hotel will be able to put you in touch with a hospital.
- Private clinics: Shanghai United Family Hospital (1139 Xianxia Lu, tel 2216 3999, shanghai.ufh.com.cn); Parkway Health (2258 Hongqiao Lu, tel 6445 5999, parkwayhealth.cn); Sino-Canadian Dental Center (Ninth People's Hospital, 639 Zhizao Julu, tel 5307 5249); Shanghai Ko Sei Dental Clinic (666 Changle Lu, tel 5404 7000).
- State hospitals: Hua Dong Hospital, Foreigners' Clinic (221 Yan'an Xilu, tel 6248 3180, ext. 3106); Huashan Hospital, Foreigners' Clinic (12 Wulumuqi Zhonglu, tel 5288 9999); IMCC in First People's Hospital (1878 Sichuan Beilu, tel 5666 3031); Pediatric Hospital, Foreigners' Clinic (Medical Center of Fudan University, 130 Yixue Yuanlu, tel 6494 1990).

MEDICINES

- Western medicines are available but can be expensive. If you have particular medical needs, make sure that you are equipped to satisfy them before you visit China.

MONEY MATTERS

- Money can be changed in most hotels. A passport may be required.
- Credit cards are accepted in international hotels, smart restaurants and tourist shops.
- RMB can be changed back into foreign currency when leaving China but you must produce relevant exchange receipts.

POST OFFICES

- The main post office is on the corner of Suzhou Beilu and Sichuan Beilu.
- Stamps can be purchased from most hotels.
- Post boxes are normally green; but you can hand your mail to the hotel receptionist.

TELEPHONES

- Local and long-distance calls can be made from the plentiful public phone boxes (coins or card) all over the city and from some newspaper kiosks.
- Local calls from hotel rooms are often free. International direct dialing is expensive. Check with your provider for cellphone charges from China; using Skype or WhatsApp is most convenient in a WiFi zone.
- The international access code from China is 00. Or call 108 to get through to a local operator in the country being called, through whom a reverse-charge call can be made.

TIPPING

- Despite official disapproval, tipping is no longer an offense. It is now expected by tourist guides, who usually prefer money—US dollars are popular—to a gift. Hotel porters will usually accept a tip, but there is no need to tip the city's taxi drivers. In most restaurants, tips are not usually expected.

TOILETS

- Western-style toilets are common in hotels and in many restaurants, but traditional squat toilets are also widely used.
- Public toilets are not generally available and those that do exist can be distinctly unsanitary. More and better facilities are gradually appearing but you are advised to carry your own paper and soap.

TOURIST OFFICES

- Shanghai has several Tourist Information and Service Centers, but they are pretty useless and are often commercially driven. It is frequently best to ask at your hotel for local information; your concierge may give you a local map and make recommendations. The following Tourist Information and Service Centers are central:

The Bund
✉ 5341 Zhongshan Dong 1-Lu ☎ 5321 0017 🕐 Daily 9.30–8

Jing'an Temple branch
✉ Lane 1678, 18 Nanjing Xilu ☎ 6248 3259 🕐 Mon–Fri 9.30–5.30

Old Town branch
✉ 149 Jiujiaochang Lu ☎ 6355 5032 🕐 Daily 9–7

Shanghai Call Centre
☎ 962288 🕐 24 hours

Language

The official language of China is known as Mandarin in the West, or *putonghua* in China, and is based on the dialect of Beijing. It is spoken throughout China but local dialects are commonly used—the Shanghai dialect is very different from *putonghua*, but locals all speak Mandarin and, as a visitor, knowledge of a few *putonghua* words and phrases will undoubtedly be an advantage at some point.

USEFUL WORDS AND PHRASES

GREETINGS

hello/how are you	*ni hao*
please	*qing*
thank you	*xiexie*
goodbye	*zai jian*
cheers!	*gan bei*
no problem	*mei wen ti*
I'm fine	*wo hen hao*
My surname is...	*wo xing...*
I am from...	*who shi laide...*

IN THE HOTEL

hotel	*binguan, fandian*
room	*fang jian*
bathroom	*weisheng jian*

POST OFFICES, BANKS AND SHOPS

post office	*youju*
stamp	*you piao*
postcard	*ming xin pian*
airmail	*hang kong*
letter	*xin*
telephone	*dianhua*
bank	*yin hang*
money exchange	*huan qian chu*
how much?	*duo shao qian?*
too expensive	*tai gui le*
a little cheaper	*pian yi dian ba*
gift	*li wu*
credit card	*xin yong ka*
antique	*gudong*
silk	*sichou*
jade	*yu*
carpet	*di tan*

EATING OUT

restaurant	*fan guan, fan dian, can ting*
Do you have a menu in English?	*You mei you ying wen cai dan?*
water/cooled	*shui/liang*
boiled water	*kaishui*
coffee	*kafei*
black tea	*hong cha*
beer	*pi jiu*
soft drink	*qi shui*
rice	*mi fan*
fork	*cha zi*
knife	*daozi*
soup	*tang*

GETTING AROUND

bus	*gong gong qi che*
bus station	*qi che zhan*
boat	*chuan*
bicycle	*zixing che*
taxi	*chu zu qi che*
train	*huo che*
toilet	*cesuo*

HEALTH

I feel ill	*wo bu shu fu*
I would like	*wo xiang*
doctor	*yi sheng*
hospital	*yiyuan*
pharmacy	*yaodian*

COLORS

black	*hei se*
brown	*he se*
pink	*fen hong se*
red	*hong se*
orange	*ju se*
yellow	*huang se*
green	*lu se*
blue	*lan se*
purple	*zi se*
white	*bai se*
gold	*jin se*
silver	*yin se*
gray	*hui se*
turquoise	*qian lan se*

DAYS/MONTHS

Monday	*Xing qi yi*	March	*san yue*
Tuesday	*Xing qi er*	April	*si yue*
Wednesday	*Xing qi san*	May	*wu yue*
Thursday	*Xing qi si*	June	*liu yue*
Friday	*Xing qi wu*	July	*qi yue*
Saturday	*Xing qi liu*	August	*ba yue*
Sunday	*Xing qi tian*	September	*jiu yue*
		October	*shi yue*
January	*yi yue*	November	*shi yi yue*
February	*er yue*	December	*shi er yue*

USEFUL WORDS

yes	*shi*	why	*wei shen me*
no	*bu*	who	*shei*
you're welcome	*bu ke qi*	may I/can I	*Wo ke yi/wo neng*
excuse me!	*dui bu qi*	open	*kai*
where	*zai na li*	closed	*guan bi*
here	*zher*	church	*jiao tang*
there	*nar*	museum	*bo wu guan*
when	*shen me shi hou*	monument	*ji nian bei*
		palace	*gong dian*

NUMBERS

0	*ling*	16	*shi liu*
1	*yi*	17	*shi qi*
2	*er*	18	*shi ba*
3	*san*	19	*shi jiu*
4	*si*	20	*er shi*
5	*wu*	21	*er shi yi*
6	*liu*	30	*san shi*
7	*qi*	40	*si shi*
8	*ba*	50	*wu shi*
9	*jiu*	60	*liu shi*
10	*shi*	70	*qi shi*
11	*shi yi*	80	*ba shi*
12	*shi er*	90	*jiu shi*
13	*shi san*	100	*yi bai*
14	*shi si*	1,000	*yi qian*
15	*shi wu*	million	*bai wan*

PRONUNCIATION

The modern phonetic romanized form of Chinese is called "pinyin". It is generally pronounced as written, but note:
a as in car
c as in bits when an initial consonant
e as in her
i as in feet unless preceded by c, ch, r, s, sh, z, sh, when it becomes er as in her
j as in gin
o as in ford
q like the ch in chin
s as in simple
u as in oo in cool
w as in wade, though pronounced by some as v
x like the sh in sheep, with the s given greater emphasis
y as in yoyo
z as ds in lids; zh as j in jam

ENGLISH

English is widely spoken in five-star hotels and in places where foreigners congregate. Generally, however, you will find that little English is spoken. A major exception is young people, who learn English at school; many of them speak at least a moderate amount of English and a growing number of young business professionals are fluent.

Timeline

THE GANGSTERS

Prewar Shanghai was an iniquitous place, fully deserving of its sobriquet as the "whore of the Orient." Nothing illustrates this better than the roles played by the gangsters, Pockmarked Huang (Huang Jinrong) and Big-eared Du (Du Yuesheng), who ran protection rackets, organized drug smuggling and controlled the city's many prostitutes. Du would warn the targets of his protection rackets of the dangers of Shanghai life by delivering a coffin to their door; Huang enjoyed perfect immunity—he was also Chief Detective for the French Sûreté.

1300s The trading center of Shanghai becomes a county seat under the jurisdiction of Jiangsu province.

1553 The people of Shanghai build a city wall during the Ming dynasty (1368–1644) to protect them from Japanese pirates.

1842 The Opium Wars reach Shanghai, which is sacked by the British. The Treaty of Nanking, signed in August, permits them to undertake unlimited trade (Concessions), in Shanghai and four other coastal cities.

1863 The British and American Concessions merge to form the International Settlement; the French Concession remains autonomous. The foreign community enjoys "extraterritoriality," which places it outside Chinese law.

1911 The Qing dynasty falls and China becomes a republic. In 1912, the city walls are demolished to create more space.

1917 Refugees from the Russian Revolution bring a new style to Shanghai entertainment—with outrageous cabarets. Shanghai emerges as the "whore of the Orient."

1927 Chiang Kai Shek is permitted by the foreign community to move troops against the Communists through the Concessions. On April 12, the Nationalists attack the Communists in Zhabei, killing 20 and arresting several hundred, including Zhou En Lai.

Below left to right: Exterior of the Museum of the First Chinese Communist Party Congress; a display in the Shanghai Museum of Chinese History; a bust of Soong Qing-ling; Mao and revolutionaries on badges at an antiques market; detail of a bronze plaque celebrating the Communist liberation of the city, at the Customs House on the Bund

1930s Japan occupies Shanghai and remains in power until the end of World War II.

1949 Mao becomes leader of the People's Republic of China and Communist troops enter Shanghai. Few foreigners remain.

1966 The Cultural Revolution begins and Shanghai, China's most industrialized and politically radical city, is the first to enter the fray. Violent rebel groups roam the streets.

1972 The Shanghai Communiqué is signed between China and the US in the Jin Jiang Hotel, signifying the end of China's isolation from the outside world.

1976 Mao dies. The Gang of Four make the city their base in their attempt to seize power.

1990s Shanghai re-enters the industrial world, becoming an autonomous municipality. Pudong is declared a Special Economic Zone and its rapid development commences.

2008 The colossal Shanghai World Financial Center is completed (▷ 94).

2016 The Shanghai Tower, China's tallest building and the world's second-tallest, opens (▷ 94).

2020 The world's largest planetarium is due to open, with a striking design incorporating an oculus, an inverted dome and a sphere.

THE GANG OF FOUR

All four members of the so-called Gang of Four, who tried to seize power following the death of Chairman Mao, had Shanghai connections. Jiang Qing, Mao's last wife, was a Shanghai actress. Chang Chun Qiao had been a journalist and director of propaganda in Shanghai. Yao Wen Yuan had been editor of the newspaper *Shanghai Liberation Army Daily*. Wang Hong Wen had been a Shanghai worker and a founder member of the Shanghai Workers Revolutionary Headquarters.

WORLD EXPO

Just two years after Beijing hosted the 2008 Olympics, China staged its first world's fair, Expo 2010, on a huge site straddling the Huangpu River (▷ 100–101). The six-month fair was attended by 73 million people, more than for any other World Expo.

Index

Shanghai 25 Best

WRITTEN BY Christopher Knowles and George McDonald
UPDATED BY Damian Harper
SERIES EDITOR Clare Ashton
COVER DESIGN Jessica Gonzalez
DESIGN WORK Liz Baldin
COLOR REPROGRAPHICS Ian Little

Published in the United Kingdom by AA Publishing.

ISBN 978-1-6409-7205-6

FIFTH EDITION

Printed and bound in China by 1010 Printing Group Limited

10 9 8 7 6 5 4 3 2 1

A05671

We would like to thank the following photographers, companies and picture libraries for their assistance in the preparation of this book.

All images are copyright AA/A Mockford & N Bonetti, except:

2/18t AA/G D R Clements; 4t AA/G D R Clements; 5 incamerastock/Alamy Stock Photo; 6cl; 6cc AA/G D R Clements; 6cr AA/D Henley; 7cl AA/G D R Clements; 7ccl AA/G D R Clements; 7ccr AA/G D R Clements; 7cr AA/G D R Clements; 7bl Paul Lee/Alamy; 10t AA/G D R Clements; 10c AA/G D R Clements; 10/11c AA/G D R Clements; 10/11b Madame Mao's Dowry; 11c AA/I Morejohn; 13bc AA/C Sawyer; 13b AA/G D R Clements; 14bc AA/A Kouprianoff; 15 Peter Treanor/Alamy Stock Photo; 16b AA/D Henley; 17t AA/G D R Clements; 17b Licensed © Robin Whalley/Alamy; 18tc AA/G D R Clements; 18c AA/G D R Clements; 20 AA/G D R Clements; 25t Damian Harper; 26l AA/G D R Clements; 26c AA/G D R Clements; 26r AA/G D R Clements; 27l AA/G D R Clements; 27r AA/G D R Clements; 28l Damian Harper; 28r Damian Harper; 29l AA/G D R Clements; 29r AA/G D R Clements; 31t AA/G D R Clements; 36r Damian Harper; 38/9 TRAVEL by VISION/Alamy Stock Photo; 39b RooM the Agency/Alamy Stock Photo; 40-41 Alamy; 41 © Kevin Foy/Alamy; 42l AA/G D R Clements; 42br AA/G D R Clements; 43t Shanghai Museum; 43bl Shanghai Museum; ; 44r Zvonimir Atletić/Alamy Stock Photo; 45bl ZUMA Press, Inc./Alamy Stock Photo; 45br AA/G D R Clements; 47 AA; 48/9 AA/I Morejohn; 50 AA/A Kouprianoff; 51 AA; 56l Tibor Bognar/Alamy Stock Photo; 56tr Jesper Haynes onasia; 56/7c AA/G D R Clements; 57tl Paul Harris onasia; 57r Licensed © Robert Harding Picture Library Ltd/Alamy; 60 jejim120/Alamy Stock Photo; 62l Fairmont Peace Hotel; 62r Fairmont Peace Hotel; 63t (Rights Managed) Gavin Hellier/Robert Harding; 63bl (Rights Managed) Gavin Hellier/Robert Harding; 63br Courtesy of Rockbund Art Museum; 65t AA/G D R Clements; 70 AA/G D R Clements; 71t MARKA/Alamy Stock Photo; 71b AA/G D R Clements; 72 Robert Wyatt/Alamy Stock Photo; 73t AA/G D R Clements; 74l AA/G D R Clements; 74r AA/G D R Clements; 75br AA/G D R Clements; 81 CHINA Landmarks and People by Vision/Alamy Stock Photo; 86 AA/G D R Clements; 87 AA/G D R Clements; 89 Prisma by Dukas Presseagentur GmbH/Alamy Stock Photo; 92 Dan Yeger/Alamy; 93t imageBROKER/Alamy; 93b Paul Lee/Alamy; 96t AA/G D R Clements; 97 AA/G D R Clements; 100tl Xinhua/Alamy; 100bl Xinhua/Alamy; 100-101 Xinhua/Alamy; 102tl AA/A Kouprianoff; 102tr AA/A Kouprianoff; 102bl AA/G D R Clements; 102br AA/G D R Clements; 103 AA/G D R Clements; 104l AA/G D R Clements; 104r AA/G D R Clements; 105-106t Panoramic Images/Robert Harding; 108/9t AA/C Sawyer; 108tcr AA; 108cbr AA/G D R Clements; 108br AA/G D R Clements; 110/112 AA/C Sawyer; 124br AA/G D R Clements; 125bl AA/G D R Clements

Every effort has been made to trace the copyright holders, and we apologise in advance for any accidental errors. We would be happy to apply the corrections in the following edition of this publication.

Titles in the Series

- Amsterdam
- Bangkok
- Barcelona
- Berlin
- Boston
- Brussels and Bruges
- Budapest
- Chicago
- Dubai
- Dublin
- Edinburgh
- Florence
- Hong Kong
- Istanbul
- Krakow
- Las Vegas
- Lisbon
- London
- Madrid
- Melbourne
- Milan
- Montréal
- Munich
- New York City
- Orlando
- Paris
- Rome
- San Francisco
- Seattle
- Shanghai
- Singapore
- Sydney
- Tokyo
- Toronto
- Venice
- Vienna
- Washington, D.C.